There Is No Blue

There Is No Blue

Martha Baillie

Coach House Books, Toronto

first edition

Published with the generous assistance of the Canada Council for the Arts and the Ontario Arts Council. Coach House Books also acknowledges the support of the Government of Canada through the Canada Book Fund and the Government of Ontario through the Ontario Book Publishing Tax Credit.

LIBRARY AND ARCHIVES CANADA CATALOGUING IN PUBLICATION

Title: There is no blue / Martha Baillie.
Names: Baillie, Martha, 1960- author.
Identifiers: Canadiana (print) 20230471242 | Canadiana (ebook) 20230471250 | ISBN 9781552454749 (softcover) | ISBN 9781770567887 (EPUB) | ISBN 9781770567894 (PDF)
Subjects: LCSH: Baillie, Martha, 1960-—Family. | LCSH: Parents—Death—Psychological aspects. | LCSH: Sisters—Death—Psychological aspects. | LCSH: Bereavement. | LCSH: Grief. | CSH: Authors, Canadian (English)—Biography. | LCGFT: Autobiographies. | LCGFT: Essays.
Classification: LCC PS8553.A3658 Z46 2023 | DDC C814/.6—dc23

There Is No Blue is available as an ebook: ISBN 978 1 77056 788 7 (EPUB), 978 1 77056 789 4 (PDF)

Purchase of the print version of this book entitles you to a free digital copy. To claim your ebook of this title, please email sales@chbooks.com with proof of purchase. (Coach House Books reserves the right to terminate the free digital download offer at any time.)

For Jonno and Emma

TABLE OF CONTENTS

Her Body

M aterials for making a death mask:

    one handful alginate
    sufficient tap water
    plaster bandages
    half a bedsheet, torn
    one plastic garbage bag, torn
    a good pound of beeswax

Tools: one large bowl, a long-handled spoon, a single-burner stove, a saucepan, an old T-shirt, a large lump of clay, fine-nosed tweezers, and any discarded implements from a dentist's office that may have come into your possession.

≈

I turned the handle and the door opened. She was sitting on the edge of her bed.

From that edge, she said, 'I've mucked this up.' She'd been looking forward to my return, but weakness and nausea prevented her from feeling as joyous as she'd hoped. She ate one of the chocolates I'd brought her, said, 'Very chocolate,' and had no appetite for a second.

May 6, 2018. Got home from Paris and went to see Mom, who tired quickly. I rarely keep a journal, except when travelling. But my mother was dying, so I kept writing.

She'd been asked during the night to 'do something with concrete objects.' They'd been 'very concrete and all flying about.' It had been 'not pleasant.'

'The sort of concrete that builders use?' I asked.

'Yes,' she confirmed, 'I'm glad you understand.' A few seconds passed, then she asked, 'What is going on outside this room where we are?' Minutes later, she tried once more to explain about the concrete objects but interrupted herself with a gesture of dismissal and the remark 'Oh, what the hell.'

Her hands and wrists were made of fine bone, wrapped in thinnest skin, stained purple in splotches here and there, stained by her blood pressing close to the surface. She used her hands to perform a small dance in the air, while lying on her back. This dance was preceded by, and illustrated, her words: 'I just don't have much get-up-and-go these days.'

She qualified her days as 'unreal.'

Cold ginger ale, sipped through a straw, soothed her nausea. She was eating very little.

She closed her eyes, opened them, and stated: 'This unreal ginger-ale existence.'

'I'm counting on you to keep me in reality,' she confided.

For years, she'd left messages on my phone: 'Hello. My name is Mary Jane and I am sitting on the edge of my bed, wondering what will happen next. You are not home, but I love you.' Always those words.

During those years, we would laugh, my husband and I. Her refusal to state her desire, to ask outright that I return her call, amused us. Her sticky indirection. Her tactic: leave hunger unspoken so it can't be measured, can't cause shame.

'I am Mary Jane. I am sitting on the edge of my bed.'

Hearing her desire to locate herself I would smile; I too was trying to locate myself, attempting to do so in language scribbled in a notebook, typed on a laptop, handed over to an editor, returned to me, and so on.

Whenever asked, 'How are you?' she would answer, 'I am here.'

She opened her eyes and announced, 'It is full of contradictions.'

'What is?'

'This treatment.'

'Your condition?'

I noticed that my hand was still holding her hand. I wondered if by 'this treatment' she meant the attention she was receiving, and meant that only by dying was she able to receive such quantities of unbroken attention from me, and from others; and I wondered if it was only her dying that allowed me to accept the intensity of her attention, her repeated attempts to locate herself through me, or, so it had often felt, her attempts to lay claim, to reclaim. By *attention*, I may mean *love*. I wrote *love*, then replaced it with the word *attention*.

When asked several years ago by a friend of mine to define love, my mother said, 'It may be that what we love we take inside ourselves, or it may be that what we love is always out there, just out of reach.'

She accepts one more spoonful of broth, parts her lips so I can slip it in. She tells me, 'I love you. I love you always,' and the full warmth, the glowing truth of her feeling, enters me. It has done so before. Every now and again it has done so – I've permitted myself to believe her. Or it has permitted me. *It* being *love*.

≈

My autonomy is being hollowed out by the suction of her death, the sweeping tug of a train entering a station, attempting to draw everyone from the platform.

≈

May 28, I had plans to go out for dinner, but when the time came, I didn't want to leave my mother, and so I texted my host to say I would not be coming. I remained seated beside the bed in which my mother lay sleeping and waking and sleeping. Around ten at night, she opened her eyes and told me, in a voice I didn't recognize, the voice of a young child rehearsing a confession: 'I'm writing a letter.'

I asked to whom.

'My last letter. I'm writing my last letter to my family.'

I asked if she'd like me to take down her words, to which she answered: 'Nope.'

'What are you telling them?' I asked.

Her answer came quickly, still in the voice of a child, a solemn child: 'That I love them all.'

I assured her that I would pass along her message, and that it would please them. She thanked me. A minute passed. Her voice had deepened when she next spoke.

'What am I to do about it?'

'About what?'

'My last days are coming.'

'Open closed open.' A fragment from a poem by Yehuda Amichai was all I had to offer. Before birth we are open to the universe, we live enclosed in our life, and when our life ends we are once more open to the universe.

'I like that,' she told me. After a moment's thought, she added, 'And then we are gone.'

Was my mother the subject or the object of the dying that occurred?

She spoke delight: 'Thank you.' 'Wonderful.' 'Yes.' 'Lovely.' Only in moments of pain: 'It hurts like hell, if you want to know the truth.'

She snored loudly the first night I slept on her floor. I lay on the gym mat one of the caregivers had brought me and listened. I read the time in large, illuminated numbers on the screen of a calendar-clock plugged into the wall. Her snoring stopped abruptly. I sat up, raised myself further until I was kneeling, and saw the soundless rise and fall of the blanket covering her chest. I leaned in, lowering my ear to her mouth, heard and felt the air enter then leave her, then I lay back down on my mat. I wondered if in the morning she'd speak, or if she'd already spoken her last words, and I tried to remember what they'd been. I lay, listening.

≈

'Who the fuck is it? Why won't you fucking tell me?'
　'Let go of my neck. Would you fucking let go?'
　Two people were coming along the footpath beneath my mother's window. Behind them was the community garden and behind it the railroad tracks and behind these the windowless red sidewall of a warehouse made of bricks. The wall separated the garden from the city's rumbling activity. A solid backdrop, it turned the area into a small stage, entered and exited by gardeners who lingered, and by passing pedestrians, and by freight trains. I was familiar with the stage set but not with the two actors now speaking, and I couldn't catch all their words. I got up from my mat and parted the curtains. They were young. He was holding

his cellphone to his ear while she shifted from one foot to the other, coming at him from behind, from right then left, reaching for his phone, demanding to know.

'Is it Jamie? Is it fucking Jamie?'

In response to his silence, she jumped on his back, wrapped her legs around his waist, her arms around his neck.

'Let go of my head. Fucking let go of my head,' he shouted, but with little anger, and tried to shake her off. Hers was the passionate, determined voice. She slid to the ground and he handed her the phone.

'Is that you, Jamie?'

The lamp on its metal pole cast a white light on the young couple, on the hard grey footpath and the lush garden – its beds bursting with kale, lettuce, zucchini, beans, tomatoes, peas – a garden where figures appeared during the day, to water and to weed, unaware that my mother was falling slowly from the sky in a corner of their tableau; absorbed in their labour, like the farmer plowing his field in Bruegel's painting of Icarus's final plunge, they worked on; and now, as the arguing young lovers exited the night scene, stage left, my mother continued her descent, unseen.

Early in the morning she opened her clouded eyes, and I described to her the moon suspended in a sky washed pink by the arrival of day, and I announced the singing of birds, whose declarations she could hear perfectly well, her ears having lost none of their acuity, and when I stopped speaking, she spoke. 'Wonderful,' she said. But this would not be her last word. She agreed to the idea of morning tea, which she consumed from the tip of a spoon.

My second night on her floor, she did not snore. I lay listening to the workings of her throat. This sound had a name. *Death rattle.* I felt the twinge of excitement and the pang of pleasure I always feel when language reveals itself to be exact, when an experience, named, finds a perfect home in words. The meaning of *death rattle* entered my ear, my chest, my belly. I lay, listening to my mother's final efforts. The excitement in me was also the excitement of death approaching, of death putting an end to waiting, an end to waiting for death to arrive.

In the morning, she opened her eyes but did not speak. I don't know if it was that morning, or the afternoon of the day before, that I cried and my tears soaked her face, and I told her I did not want her to leave, I did not want her life to end, that I would miss her terribly, and she opened and closed her mouth but could express her alarm with her eyes only, and I stopped myself and told her, still sobbing, that her love would make me strong, always, and her face relaxed.

The unrehearsed. What we think we will say and what we say. Her Tibetan caregiver had warned me, sternly, while we were changing my mother's diaper the day before: 'Your tears are not what she needs.' I'd weighed her warning, uncertain.

There had been times when I'd looked at her and wanted my freedom. I could not count the number of times I'd longed to be free of her, my mother, the one who worried and watched and hovered at the edge of me, asking, asking. Or so I thought. What had she been asking?

≈

While my mother was dying, my sister found and gave to me a square notebook, its cover made of brown leather, worn thin along the spine, 'Compliments of the Egyptian

Chemical Company' stamped in tiny gold letters in the bottom left corner. My grandfather had sold desk calendars, agendas, and other office items, for Brown & Bigelow. Likely, the Egyptian Chemical Company had been one of his clients. Most of the pages my mother had left blank, then came sketched heads of women, several of an older woman, all in pencil, followed by more emptiness, more silence, a half-page of writing, silence again, then several pages of words, and a newspaper clipping dated June 10, 1947. So, it was two years since the war had ended, and seven since she'd graduated from college and had begun painting, and had moved to Gloucester, Massachusetts, then New York, when she'd written:

> this grey street corner. But around it is hovering a spring-laden wind. Where am I?

≈

I am still asking myself if I saw her die or saw death arrive and take her. It twisted her face. It forced her to grin: a Halloween grin that stretched her lips and exposed her teeth. Quick, sharp, it raised her shoulders twice before it let go. The two friends who'd arrived minutes before, and who'd stood beside me while death gripped my mother, now stepped out into the hall.

She looked as if she were taking a nap. I kissed her forehead and with the tips of my fingers tried to memorize the shape of her nose, eyes, cheeks, and chin. I sat and looked out the window at the garden, where figures were bending, weeding, and watering. Breeze and birdsong entered. Time stirred. I looked again at my mother. I tapped the screen of my phone and called my daughter in Montreal. We spoke. I tapped the screen of my phone and called my friend Iris, who knew how to make a death mask, Iris, who is rarely at home, more likely in her studio, or in bed with one of several lovers, or digging a hole in her backyard, or waiting at an airport. She picked up the phone.

'What are you up to?' I asked.

'I'm drinking my morning coffee.'

'Have you got a full day ahead of you? A lot planned?'

'No. Amazing, eh? I've been crazy busy, but I've saved today. The whole day. Nothing. All of it for me. And you? How are you? Where are you?'

'I'm sitting beside my mother. She's just died.'

≈

I am not writing about Iris. I am writing about my mother, but because she is dead and life is continuing, she is being covered over by words about the living. Even in this narrative, the telling of her death, the living are nudging their way to the front. Don't blame Iris. I asked her to use her skills, and she said, 'Yes. I'll have to look and see if I have all the materials,' and she got on her bicycle and an hour later arrived at the door to my mother's room.

Minutes before Iris arrived, two caregivers knocked, came in, explained that it was time to wash my mother. I said I wanted to wash her. They handed me the washcloth. It was warm and damp. Soap must have been added to the water because bubbles floated in the plastic basin they'd brought in. I lifted my mother's arm. My washcloth-covered hand discovered parts of my mother's body I did not remember having ever touched before, although I imagine I did touch almost all of her when I was a very young child and her body was my territory. Only a few white hairs grew from her armpit, from that soft and shallow pit. Her breasts, a bit more generous than my tiny ones, spread out, two flattened confections, a pretty pink nipple in the centre of each. The skin of her breasts and belly had a loveliness that shocked and delighted me. I was used to her being vertical when naked, not horizontal, her belly and breasts hanging, while she stood or sat and I changed her clothes. In her present position of repose, of complete stillness, an inexplicable youthfulness returned to her breasts and belly – an innocence, as if they'd never known effort. They had an effortless beauty. My washcloth-wrapped fingers moved down from her belly and along the lips of her vagina, cleaned all around the opening. This opening had been my father's entrance into her and my exit from her. Through this opening in my mother, I'd first entered the world, the world outside her. Two months have passed, and the memory of washing my mother is becoming the idea of washing my mother. But when I touched my mother between her legs, touched the place of my entrance into the world, a memory came to me of a borderless time. It was a bodily recollection of knowing no separation. I was touching this place of knowing for a second and last time. The wonder and peace I felt as I touched her there were replaced almost at once by sadness and longing, and already I was moving my hand down her leg, and soon we were heaving her onto her side, so I could clean her back and slide my hand down to her backside, where, the caregiver warned, there was feces.

Her calves and ankles I did not wash. The slightest abrasion, the least rubbing, and her purple shins and ankles might have bled. The day before, the nurse had fastened padded bracelets around her ankles, bracelets we now removed. I decided she had no need of socks but took from her wardrobe a pair of black pants, a short-sleeved white shirt, and a black, much-embroidered jacket, upon which a garden of flowering plants, in gold, green, blue, and mauve, had been stitched; it was the costume she'd chosen and planned to wear to her hundredth-birthday celebration, which had formed a hazy horizon she'd often gazed toward.

'What do you want to do for your birthday?'

'I want lots of champagne. I want everyone to drink lots of champagne.'

We'd begun washing my mother when Iris arrived. She set her bag of materials on a chair. When one of the caregivers was called away, Iris helped hold my mother on her side while I traced my mother's spine with my washcloth-clad hand.

My mother bathed and dressed, I closed the door behind the caregivers. I looked down at my mother. Her upside-down smile came to her from her mother, a smile of quiet, conspiratorial amusement; the heavily hooded eyes and strong nose she'd received from her father. There was a hollow in her left cheek, where a cancer had been dug out.

What we were about to do, Iris assured me, would not alter my mother's appearance. First, we spread pieces of plastic over the exposed areas of pillow and over the upper portion of my mother's jacket, bringing the plastic right up to the edges of her face. With the torn sheet we did the same, tightly encircling her face with white fabric so that now my mother resembled a nun. A few white hairs escaped her cowl at her forehead. These we smoothed and coated with Vaseline. Into her nostrils we inserted small plugs of compressed Kleenex. The alginate, once mixed with water, would solidify quickly. As we emptied the contents of the bowl onto her face, drowning her in a thick pink brightness, already the alginate's startling Kool-Aid colour was shifting to ghost white. We held it close, to prevent it from sliding away. Once it had firmed into a rubbery substance that captured on the outside the shape of our hands and on the inside her features, we paused. We cleaned the bowl and our hands. She lay with her face covered. The plaster bandages we could apply slowly as they would take fifteen to twenty minutes to dry. The plaster's function was to provide a strong shell for the alginate mould to rest in, once we'd peeled it from her face.

Waiting for the plaster to harden, we ate. We were hungry and so we ate. I was tired and drank from a Thermos of tea. The day was becoming hot. Through the open window came sounds of activity. A car engine. A bird. We turned to face the window. My back to my mother, I ate. To chew and swallow in the presence of my dead mother troubled me. My behaviour struck me as disrespectful. The discomfort I felt was the discomfort I'd experience, I imagine, were I to eat while standing in front of a painting of great beauty and power, a work capable of altering those who give it their full attention. Or perhaps I did not believe she was dead, and believed instead that I should offer her some of my food and drink but knew she would refuse my offer. To eat and drink confronted me with a contradiction, a suspicion lodged in me, that she was at once dead and not dead, that she could be both the one and the other.

Carefully we separated the rubbery substance from her face, lifting the white shape, cutting it free wherever an edge of the sheet had caught. My mother reappeared. She wore the same look of quiet amusement as before.

Iris placed the rubbery mould in its plaster shell, the two in a box, the box in her bicycle basket, and rode away. I remained with my mother.

I sat with her and waited. I did not know what I was waiting for. I'd been told I could decide when to have her body removed. Once my mother left her bed, she would next lie in the interior of a large refrigerator. I waited. While I was waiting, my husband arrived and sat with me, and together we sat with my mother and waited. At some point I stood up, stepped closer, and looked at her hands. I did this because I was missing her hands. They were the last part of her body with which she'd been able to express herself. Once her eyes had closed and her mouth gone mute, still she'd been able to rearrange her hands on her chest. I saw now that her fingers were becoming a pale yellow and that the tip of each finger was being invaded, under the nail, by a cloud of bluish mauve. 'You've been swimming too long,' I could hear her telling me. 'It is time to come out. The lake is cold. You'll catch a chill.' I tried to lift her arm but it resisted, locked in place. The skin of her forehead left a clammy dampness on my fingers. To this body I could attach the word *corpse*.

Into my cellphone I did not speak the word *corpse*, but it was this unspoken word inside my head that allowed me to ask them to come take away the body, her body.

A man and a woman came. They knocked, then opened the door. Words of condolence came out of the man's mouth as if on a roll of paper, the paper that spills from a cash register when numbers are entered. I did not want this man to touch my mother. Before I could stop him, he reached out and I heard a loud cracking sound as he bent my mother's arm. In answer to my objection, he informed me that to break the rigor mortis was standard procedure. I told him I did not see the point of what he'd done, since he could have fit her perfectly well into a box without having altered the position of her arm and that, in any case, she was to be cremated. I did not argue further because the violence had been done and could not be undone, and I did not want to argue in front of my mother. Together the three of us lifted her from her bed. We placed her in a bag and zipped the bag closed, as if it were a snowsuit, a black velvet snowsuit, then strapped her onto the gurney they'd wheeled into her room. The velvet of the bag was meant to convince me that the funeral home considered my mother's body to be a precious object, an object they would not lose, or give away, or sell, or break. Over the bag they spread a small blanket, to give the impression to any elderly resident we might pass in the hallway that she was sleeping and on her way to a hospital to be cured. I could think of no other reason for the small crocheted blanket. An elevator carried us down. In the underground garage, the hearse waited. They slid my mother in and asked if I'd care to close the door on her, which I did.

≈

In her studio, Iris heated a pound of beeswax in a saucepan. It was old wax, from an earlier project, now being recycled, and she threw in a few candle stubs she had lying about. Once the wax had liquefied, she poured it through a T-shirt several times, straining out every bit of soot. Any soot not removed would have sunk to the lowest part of my mother's face, would have blackened the tip of her nose. The hard plaster shell, containing the alginate mould, Iris placed face down on a mound of damp clay. She made sure that the face, about to become a vessel, was level and that it would not move. The hot wax, as it poured into the mould, smelled sweet.

It would have been best to separate the solid wax from the mould that evening, but Iris had not planned to spend her evening making a death mask, and so she went out as she'd planned to do. By morning, the alginate had stuck in places to the mask. She peeled most of it off and removed the remaining traces as best she could using tweezers and a needle. Not all could be removed. Rather than risk damaging the finished mask, she left fine lines of white within a few folds in the wax.

≈

To burn my mother – to melt her flesh, and to alter her bones so these might be ground into the granular substance called 'ashes' to be poured into a jar – would require that the heat enveloping her rise to between 1,400 and 1,800 degrees Fahrenheit. The furnace was turned off when I arrived. My mother's corpse waited in a closed wooden box, inside a closed cardboard box, in front of the square mouth of the furnace, a mouth with a metal door. From two hooks in the wall, to the left of the furnace, hung a helmet with a golden visor and a space-age silver jacket. This was the shimmering armour to be worn by the knight who would tend my mother's burning body, who would reach into the heat with the long tongs now resting against the wall and rearrange her bones so that these be consumed more completely.

He stood, now, to one side, waiting while attempting not to appear to be waiting. This performance of patient discretion was part of his job. We were all performing. Following a death, roles are assigned. He was a short man, sinewy, no extra flesh on him, his pants a size too large, his belt pulled tight. The knuckles of his small hands were large, and the hair on his head thin. I sensed a silence in him that was not part of his performance, a silence that was his own, and I was grateful for it. His uneasy look, of a man being pursued and refusing to run, made me warm to him. I often feel that I am being pursued, and sometimes I run whereas other times I don't. His name was Paul, I later learned, and he lived in a room above the cemetery office. He'd acquired the craft of cremating bodies not in a classroom but in the room where we now stood, a room with walls of thick stone and a low ceiling, a room built into a low hill. On top of us sat the Chapel of St. James-the-Less.

When I indicated that I was ready for him to begin cremating my mother, he walked over to the furnace, bent down, picked up two short tubes made of stiff cardboard that were lying ready on the ground, and set these in the mouth of the furnace. On two cardboard tubes, my mother, inside her box, would roll forward. Paul slid her into the furnace; he gave a final shove, to either her feet or her head. I wanted to know if she was leaving feet first or head first but did not ask. I had so many questions, small questions. The answers would have been as small as grains of sand, and together they might have added up to a large answer, an answer large enough to stand on and stare out to sea. Paul pressed the button that lowered the metal door.

A plume of black smoke rose out of the chimney. Briefly, my mother marked the blue sky. By the time I'd come around the front of the chapel and stood on the path running the length of its north side, my mother had become transparent vapour. Crossing the path, she undulated, visible, as rippling light.

Before the burning of my mother had begun, I'd arrived at the cemetery on my bicycle, which I'd locked to the tall iron fence. For the past few days, the city, as I moved through it, had looked new to me, as if I were seeing the buildings, the parks, the layout of the streets for the first time. Why the city of my birth, where I'd lived all my life, should strike me as new, I could not explain. Perhaps I was seeing it as my mother had seen it when she'd married my father and first moved here; perhaps I was returning to the start of her story. But this made no sense since that old city (once new to her) no longer existed and was not the city passing before my eyes. The sensation of newness I was experiencing was being caused, nonetheless, by my mother. I felt certain of this.

A Bend in the Path

Is it losing my mother that is making me want to lure my father back into the present? Twenty-five years ago, I was pregnant, preoccupied, then suddenly my father was gone. He'd vanished into a hole in the ground. The hole was lined with unrequested bright plastic grass rolled out and down to prevent our eyes from seeing soil embrace the shiny box that held him.

Weeks later my child was born, a daughter. Within the first hour of her life outside my body, she raised one eyebrow and gave me a look so skeptical that I thought my father had returned.

My daughter's exit (from within me) and her entry (into a room full of air and sunlight) had been speedy, and had caused me no unbearable pain as I braced my foot against the midwife's shoulder. For this extraordinary fact I thanked my father. I'd been spared the agony childbirth so often imposes; gratitude to something or someone was in order. I could have thanked my daughter but we'd not yet met, not face to face. The midwife had caught her and was now cleaning and swaddling her.

Bestowing thanks on my father made him present in the room where my husband and my mother, minutes before, had witnessed a tiny new person shoot free from between my thighs. My daughter appeared healthy and vigorous. Fleetingly I imagined that my father had interceded, that he'd eased his first grandchild's voyage, that he'd done so using special powers acquired by dying. This idea pleased me. It felt fitting.

One afternoon, when I'd dropped by my parents' house, he'd placed his hands on the fabric of my distended summer dress and had said, bending low, addressing the infant growing inside me: 'You don't know me, and I'll never meet you, but I love you.'

Hearing his words, I'd understood that he knew the cancer ravaging his body would kill him within a month or two. The truth of his imminent departure could no longer be sequestered to a corner of my mind. That afternoon I mourned him. But my ability to deny reality was quickly restored, and I continued to believe that he would live forever.

I was not the one looking after him, accompanying him to a grinding number of medical appointments. My mother saw to all that. My sense of their daily lives was conveniently vague. They'd both 'always' lived in the house of my birth, available when I needed them, leaving me free, in the decades since I'd left that house, to attempt to grow up and get on with my own life. And when they were not in that house in the city, I could find them a two-hour drive away, in a cabin perched on an open hillside overlooking woods that descended into a valley. Or I could find them on one of the many winding paths my father had made through those woods.

≈

I've come to my parents' cabin with a large box of my father's letters, a smaller box of snapshots from his youthful travels, and a third box containing the jar holding my mother's ashes – her finely ground, fire-altered bones.

Today, rain is falling on the sloping fields. Rain is moving in vertical sheets. All week rain has kept coming, just as it did the week before.

One day, wind will clear the sky and I'll take the jar holding my mother and release her at the exact spot on the path where my father said she should come to look for him if she wanted to meet him after his death.

I don't know if my mother, during the twenty-five years she outlived my father, ever went to visit him at the spot he'd chosen. Nonetheless I will take her to that dipping bend in the path and empty her from her jar, on whatever day the rain lets up.

That none of the letters I've pulled, so far, from the large box of dishevelled time at my feet have been addressed to my mother does not mean that my father didn't love her. He adored her. Less certain, for me, is how she felt about him or about anyone. She was skilled at waiting and observing. She'd been a silent and serious child, who stared through thick glasses and was much teased for resembling an owl. She'd learned to be cautious and calculating in her responses to others. In contrast, my father allowed his thoughts and emotions to pour freely, all too often unedited.

A delicate blue envelope has just surfaced. On it my father's name, in my mother's hand. Also the address of the house of my childhood and adolescence and young adulthood. She must be away from home, if she's writing to him. I snatch up the envelope. Likely she's visiting her mother in the New Hampshire countryside, and likely she has taken us – the two children – with her.

'Darling, my darling … I'm writing now on the screen porch where it is lovely and cool after the hot humid day. The thrushes are singing – and most of all I wish you were here with me!'

My mother's voice singing to my father, singing clearly in my ear, as if she were perched on one of the bare branches outside this cabin window. A sudden joy opens wide inside me. I continue to read.

But reading other people's letters exacts a price. On the following page comes more evidence of intimacy between my parents. This time their intimacy takes the form of a shared joke, their source of amusement my inability to spell, a failing that filled me with shame and rage as a child.

'The girls are next door playing Scrabble ... Martha wouldn't let me see but only read to me her card to "Dear Dady," but when you get it you may wonder what kind of Scrabble game it can be next door! I suspect Martha will end up keeping score! But she certainly can draw!'

Having read what wasn't mine to read, I've tasted both the tenderness my mother expressed to my father in private and her lighthearted mockery of me – both these flavours are now mine to savour. The letter is postmarked 1971, so my sister would have been thirteen and I eleven.

I was twenty-one when I stopped spelling *sompthing* the way it sounded to my ear. For several decades my mind's reluctance to retain the shapes of words on a page, to recall the exact composition of letters forming a given word, caused me grief, which early on I translated into defiance. Spelling was an abyss to be crossed on an aural tightrope.

≈

Tomorrow the weather will shift, promises a voice on the radio.

≈

Once, looking out this window, my father said that when he died he wanted to be placed in a plain plywood box and lowered into a hole dug at the bottom of the hill, so that the minerals held within him might quickly return to soil familiar to him and feed the saplings laying claim to the hillside. But such a burial would be illegal, he warned, and must remain a dream.

His dream sends me away from the window to look for a poem by Jack Davis, 'Variations on the Decomposing

Fox.' From the poem's middle, these lines pronounce the beauty of returning our body's borrowed riches:

The earth inoculates
this crowded second
ensoulment and inheld

breath now home
to a commotional
solitude

of microbial longueurs

≈

Many of the letters in the cardboard box at my feet are dated 1936 to 1938 and were sent by my father to his parents. Reports of student life in vibrant New York, offered to family stuck in staid Toronto. Though war is approaching, it goes unmentioned. Girls, food, entertainment, assignments, lectures, and stretching his fellowship money occupy his mind.

I know more about his future than he does. At last I am the one who knows more. This pleases me. It also makes me wish I could protect him. He is so very young – twenty-one. A tall fellow, lean but broad shouldered, with a long head, a cleft in his chin, and dark brown eyes set too close together for his liking, their closeness a flaw he notes when studying his face in the mirror, as he must do each morning to shave.

The day of his arrival in New York he proudly reports having found his way, by subway and on foot, then briefly in a taxi, from Grand Central Station to a Columbia University residence, John Jay Hall, at 511 West 114th Street.

Having unpacked, he showers but cannot get the water cold enough to give a 'proper finish' to his 'tough hide.' He regrets having brought neither soap nor a change of underwear.

I know this man's body. I read his words and picture his nakedness. I am no longer, but will always be, the child who laid claim to his body by leaping up into his arms or falling onto his chest. Riding on his shoulders, I grasped his forehead while his hands clasped my ankles, and before me the horizon tilted to the rhythm of his steps. In anger I beat his body with my fists. In happiness I scratched his naked back so that he'd scratch mine, and after several minutes I'd remark on the unfairness that my hands were small and his back large, while his hands were large and my back small, which made his contribution to our exchange lesser.

Admiring the movement of the long muscles in his calves as he walked, I strived to match his stride. We meandered through woods, he teaching me the names of trees. We descended through waist-deep, tangled growth – grass, thistle, chicory, and burdock. Our boots removed, we compared our feet, pressing them into the ground and wriggling our toes. Fingers spread out, we compared hands. That my legs and arms, feet and hands, replicated his in miniature and bore little resemblance to my mother's delighted me.

I keep reaching into his letters, hoping to find the intimate father I hear and see in my head, but I encounter bravado – the flaunting of a newly minted masculinity by someone not yet free of the need, or desire, to confess to his parents his every triumph and woe.

I find it easy to love this young man, though some of his vocabulary – *hussy*, *slut*, *vixen*, *witch*, and *Golden Beauty*

– makes me wince. He exudes an open eagerness. I know well his lack of sophistication, his overblown self-confidence tempered by anxious self-doubt, his honesty, warmth, and curiosity. His thoughtfulness and thoughtlessness, his laziness and self-discipline, are familiar to me. I know in my bones his fear of spending money.

Grown older, he'll bend to place a dramatic kiss on the hand of a woman his age (a friend of our mother's?) or on the hand of a teenaged friend of mine, in a performance of gallantry intended to amuse, a pantomime that suggests men may be needed to protect women, and that bestowing on men the authority of guardian might benefit all.

Yet it was my mother who 'saved' my father. Often, as I grew, he'd announce: 'Your mother saved me from a life of loneliness.' He'd lived forty-one years by the time she rescued him.

≈

I've pulled another letter from the box and am admiring the generous shape of each vowel, the fluid motion of his hand.

His passion is mathematics, but his subject, at Columbia, economics – a field rapidly disillusioning him.

At the end of two years he'll choose to return home without the doctorate he set out to obtain. He'll be offered, nonetheless, a position teaching at his alma mater, the University of Toronto. He'll slip back into the familiar, but no longer able to pass for a prodigy.

≈

I am small and in bed with my father, asking him questions, or tickling his ribs, or examining his chin and nose and ears, when the phone rings. I slide to the floor, dash to the lowest bookshelf, where the black phone sits with its round dial, lift the heavy receiver from its cradle, and ask, 'Hello?' The deep male voice may belong to my uncle – 'Is your father up, or is the old slob still in bed?'

I bristle, hold the receiver away from my ear, and stare at my father.

'Who is it?' he asks, sitting himself up.

I name my uncle, then pause, hesitant to reveal the cutting words but too angry to conceal them.

'He says you're a slob.' My father's laughter fills the room as he asks me to pass the phone. *Never will I forgive you*, I silently hiss into the receiver – into my uncle's ear – as I hand the heavy black device to my incomprehensibly smiling father.

Of his three older brothers, closest in age to my father was 'Uncle Pete,' whose real name was James. Two and a half years separated the two. In grade school my father, in one prodigious leap, landed in the same class as James. Teachers, who regarded humiliation as a prime pedagogical tool, pounced on any failure by James to provide a correct answer. They called on Donald, his younger brother. They praised my father, and to James recommended emulation. Outside the classroom, my uncle took revenge, mocking my father's lack of aptitude whenever a ball was to be caught, kicked, or hit with a bat, or a race to be won, or a dance step learned.

A fraught affection tied the two. They'd test each other and both pass the test. They shared an acquired habit of mockery, and when addressing each other used language to express the opposite of their actual thoughts, and to conceal their true feelings.

≈

Thanks to our father: a roof, clothing, and food. Yet it is our mother who selects our clothes, washes and mends them, and prepares our food. Thanks to our father: money. To provide for us he makes himself absent. When my sister and I return from school always our mother is there, always our father at work. He returns in time for dinner, and dinner is followed by more work. Then comes the weekend and, thanks to our father: foolishness – a sudden who-cares-what-anyone-thinks – wild charades, pantomimes, board games, and ballads belted out of tune. Or off he goes into the woods, and my sister and I follow, then veer away, tugged by the allure of our own explorations, accompanied sometimes by our mother but more often by our friends, as we grow. Thanks to our father: self-discipline, and self-recrimination.

≈

I reach back into the cardboard box, convinced I'll find some mention of approaching war. Instead I discover him climbing out his thirteenth-floor bedroom window onto a stone ledge. New York spreads far below. It is a long way down. The year is 1936. He and his soulmate, Joe, sit in their underwear on the ledge, discussing girls, 'talking the situation over,' and 'letting things slide.' A full moon hangs above the Hudson.

At last a photo, clipped from a newspaper, rewards my curiosity. Women dressed in identical narrow grey skirts, dark blouses and caps, stand at attention before a grinning and uniformed man, who clasps his hands behind his back as he inspects and praises, as he moves along the row the women form. Under the photo, the heading: 'British M.P. Hints Ban on Political Uniforms.' Below this heading, a brief text clarifies: 'Sir Oswald is shown inspecting girl members of the Union of British Fascists. He is wearing the swank redesigned uniform which marked him and his fellow members a few days after he was creditably reported to have received new and substantial backing from an unknown … ' Whoever wielded the scissors has eliminated the rest of the text about British fascism and Sir Oswald Mosley, while leaving intact an advertisement for shampoo: 'A dash of Dandrine daily will keep your hair so clean it will fairly shine.'

I flip the clipping, find a photo of young men, uniformed, throwing themselves on top of each other – a 'heap of bone and brawn.' Dressed in immaculate white, the referee blows his whistle. A blurred crowd cheers from the bleachers: ' … the first touchdown for Varsity in the game with McGill at Varsity Stadium this afternoon … '

Someone (my grandfather?) has triumphantly added in pen: 'Final score: 35–1.' University football is presumed of interest in my father's family, his oldest brother, while studying medicine at U of T, having risen to stardom on the Varsity team.

My father, awkward on his feet, took up rowing.

≈

The boat is long and slender, blue on the inside, yellow on the outside. Cast in fibreglass, modelled on the boat he rowed as a student, but adapted to hold a family of four, it binds his past to his present. August has arrived and we've fled the city for an island in a lake. A set of oars has been purchased for my sister Christina and me. Positioned side by side, on the smooth blue seat in front of our father, we brace our feet (as best we can) on the bottom of the boat. Each pulls on her oar. Mine jumps from its lock, slams the gunnel, and slides. I declare my frustration. Calmly our father encourages. But his tone is amused. Again I pull, lose patience, and refuse.

At dusk my father tugs on his yellow oars. They are immense and extend from his body. In each stroke I feel his strength propel the boat. It is carrying us over the water. Our mother rides serene in the stern. She faces us, her look of repose foreign to my agitation. Beside me, my sister too sits serene. The stillness of the lake, the gliding boat, the softness of the air sliding over my face, and the creaking of the oars: these smooth my emotions. I scan the water as my sister is doing. The first to spot the small dark animal head, and the rippling V of its wake, gestures with her arm, pointing wordlessly so as not to reveal our presence. Then comes the slap of the beaver's broad tail. We've been detected despite the thickening darkness enveloping us.

≈

As a teenager I asked my father why he'd chosen to enlist in the Navy. Democracy needed defending, he answered. But why the Navy? He'd hoped to die a clean, quick death, he said. The cold of the Atlantic would kill him fast. No drowning in mud, in a rat-infested trench stinking of putrefaction. No mustard gas to burn his lungs.

At age eleven, he, along with his classmates, in 1926, had attributed the behaviour of two teachers to time spent in the trenches of World War I. The one who suffered from fits of coughing they suspected had been gassed, while shell shock explained the jumpiness of the other. This second teacher, an astonishing marksman, could hit a boy in the head with a flying piece of chalk, barely turning from the blackboard to aim. My father used such boyhood tales to explain his choice of the Navy.

The only boats he truly loved were rowboats. He hoped to never again be surrounded by the grey Atlantic and have to gaze at its infinite expanse for weeks on end.

I wanted him to have been a hero. No, he insisted, quite the opposite. From the outset he'd made serious mistakes. Early on he'd selected the wrong kind of cable for the radar equipment of which he was in charge. When a drum of lead-covered, unbending cable came on board in Gibraltar, it was too late to get hold of the flexible kind needed for the radar aerials to rotate. When ordering supplies, he'd made a single letter error in the Admiralty Pattern Number.

Two years later, haggling inside a depot in Alexandria, trying to obtain as many precious cathode ray tubes as possible, he'd heard a ship blow its horn and had paid no attention. Rommel was advancing dangerously close and so British ships were pulling out in haste, heading for the relative safety of Haifa or Port Said. Focused on his task, he'd continued to bargain with the man in charge of the depot. Again the call of a ship's horn. This time the sound took hold and fear struck. His own ship was pulling out. He ran from the depot, raced in a car along the corniche, hailed a felucca, was rowed swiftly out. Having caught up with his ship, which had not yet picked up speed, he was able to board by climbing a lowered ladder, his bundle of tubes and other spare parts clutched under his arm. He anticipated a severe reprimand but was spared because of the supplies he'd secured.

≈

From the cardboard box I've pulled another letter, this one penned on a very small piece of thin paper.

HMS *Cormorant*
11th May 1943

Dear Baillie,

I understand that you have written to the Bristol Hotel regarding your greatcoat recently.

In response to your letter of 6th February I packed the greatcoat in a CB bag with other effects and put it aboard the Sidi Ifni explaining to Lieut. C. S. Irwin RNR where to take it. It was labeled exactly as the address given by you at the heading of your letter.

For security reasons I cannot give further information but I suggest that you make enquiries at your end, and trust you will be able to trace it.

Yours,

DB Jarrett

Paymaster. Captain's Secretary

He's lost his greatcoat, my absentminded not-yet-father.

As a young child I found his greatcoat. I pulled it down from its hanger in the front hall closet. Lured by its brass buttons, I tried it on and paraded from room to room in search of an audience, much of the coat dragging on the floor and the rest of it swallowing me.

A uniform, I was sternly informed, was not a costume, not a plaything. The heavy coat with its two shiny rows of buttons and two gold ribbons (or three?) wound round its lower sleeve was returned to the closet to hang in eternal darkness.

≈

Trees, he'd tell me, hurt no one. They are the lungs of the world. Until today, I imagined it was war – the fear of being attacked from below by a submarine or strafed from above by an enemy plane – that compelled him to plant trees in great number.

But having set aside the large box holding his letters, I've pulled from the shoebox containing his photos an image of ugliness and destruction taken before the war, summer of 1938, in Tennessee – a portrait of a bare hill. Deeply pleated by erosion, it resembles an atrophied brain. Two forlorn houses crown the monstrously infertile mound. On the back my father has written, 'Erosion at Ducktown. The social wages of a free rein to the profit motive.'

≈

A shack, built just big enough to enclose a camping cot and pot-bellied stove. He hammered together this rough shelter and covered it in green shingles so he could stay overnight, and the next morning continue planting trees. Discharged at the end of the war, he'd resumed teaching mathematics and purchased fifty acres of land. Weekdays he lived in the city with his parents. Weekends he devoted to trees.

The Men of the Trees, the Tree Bee (a tree identification contest between teams of students from schools across the city): into these organizations he threw himself.

When he was not thinking of trees or mathematics or women or family, the suffering of animals preoccupied him.

'You all know that your dog or cat certainly doesn't like to have his paws trod on. If you want a rough idea of the leg-hold trap, just imagine that the door of your car has been slammed across the fingers of your bare hand. Imagine that the car door is jammed shut – and imagine that you are then left with your hand so caught until you either starve to death or freeze to death – or you tear apart your hand,' he urges in a letter published in a rural paper.

Seated in a booth at a fair, he handed out pamphlets and offered to demonstrate the speed and force of the newly patented Conibear body trap, designed to quickly kill. The year was 1957.

'It's in your own publications,' he told any trapper who'd listen, 'that I've learned that 20 percent of animals caught in leg-hold traps, every season, succeed in freeing themselves by gnawing or twisting off their paw.'

≈

Smoothing the small square of thin paper, rereading Paymaster Jarrett's brief response to my father's request, in 1943, for assistance recovering his greatcoat, I hear my mother ask, a smile forming on her lips, 'But didn't you take the car this morning?'

We are at dinner and my father's been describing a peculiar passenger seated across from him on the Bathurst bus, in which he rode home from work. 'You're right,' he agrees, shaking his head, bemused, and attempts to recall where on the university campus he parked the car, which will remain there overnight.

From him my absentmindedness. From him my short temper. From him my arms and legs, my hands and feet, my dark eyes, and my nose.

I can reach inside me and touch a closeness and ease that once were ours – my father's and mine. Our physical intimacy feels as distant as childhood, and as potent.

I descend into the woods, and the language of tree bark and leaves surrounds me.

≈

Long before he died he started to withdraw. Years of arguments with my sister had made him wary. As a teenager she'd become a puzzle he couldn't solve, and this had angered him. If a key to her existed he couldn't find it. Instead he made her cry. And our mother, hearing her daughter's tears, fixed him with an angry gaze, and he too wanted to cry.

There was a language he spoke that I did not care to understand, certain it could bring me no pleasure. Within mathematics he lived apart from the three of us, who shared a home with him. Within mathematics my mother could no more join him than he could encounter her within her art.

In the car, me driving, by then in my twenties, he in the passenger seat, wooded hills and open fields sailing by on either side, the car carrying us forward, he'd ask me to explain the workings of our family and I'd marvel that he, the smart one, the mathematician, understood so little. Listening to my words he'd shake his head in admiration and thank me, as if I were performing some extraordinary feat of translation. Some conversations can take place only in a car.

Coming out of the hospital the three of us – he, my mother, and I, Christina left inside in the psych ward, after her first suicide attempt in her twenties – I slipped my arm through his, but he freed himself, saying, 'You are grown now and shouldn't be turning to your father for closeness.' He'd become scared to touch me or to be touched by me. He was, said my sister, the cause of her desire to die.

≈

You Can Say Goodbye

1

One day, in August, or at the very end of July, my sister wrote on her bedroom wall – or perhaps she did so at night. In blue marker, in calm cursive, she gave three reasons to die. Her final poem: three rungs of words on the vertical white surface.

Her intention wasn't to climb up or down her ladder of language. She didn't believe in heaven or hell, except here, in the 'human' world.

Because of schizophrenia
Because of The Juniper Tree
Because of losing the house

And a dozen inches lower, off to the right, in block letters:
YOU CAN SAY GOODBYE.

In the kitchen, she left a second message: two small canvases propped upright on the cluttered counter. On the canvas to the left, a head in profile, executed in black, filled to bursting with tangled brush strokes. This portrait of her torn and raging mind, this roar of pain, she connected by a short arrow to the words 'C'est moi.' On the canvas to the right, white paint, carefully applied to create a square of welcoming silence. Of licence. Paired paintings proposing a sideways exit, a short leap from left to right – out of agony into stillness of death. The year was 2019. She'd lived sixty-one years.

One day, in August, we found what remained of her. I waited until ten in the morning that day before cycling over to see if she'd taken the note I'd taped, the day before, to the front door. By ten, the air was hot, humid, thick. If Christina was going to venture out on such a sticky summer day, she'd do so early and see my note. I rode over the uneven flagstones of the path leading from the road to the front steps, slipped off my bicycle, and leaned it against the side of the house. Behind the hydrangeas in the front garden the air conditioner sat. No motor sound, no whirring blades. The silence of the air conditioner and its motionless blades made my heart race. Only rarely in summer did she turn off the air conditioner. I hurried up the steps.

I'd decided that if my note was still taped to the door, I must knock, I must do exactly what she'd asked me to not do: intrude.

There it was, my note, suspended from the bit of tape securing it to the door. She'd not stepped outside, not noticed the dangling envelope. She'd neither read my words nor torn them into unread pieces.

The air smelled foul. I lifted the lid of the large municipal recycling bin, which she kept by the front door. When she'd left it by the side door, a neighbour had filled it with his own plastic and paper waste, and when I'd asked if she wanted me to speak with him, she'd said no, that once already she'd wheeled the bin over and emptied it in the road in front of his driveway, in her fury, and now the best solution was for her to simply keep it by the front door, even if this meant more physical effort and inconvenience for her; she'd rather avoid a confrontation, she said, while still stopping him from using her bin, because if he continued to take advantage of her, she might lose her temper again, and her next retaliation could be worse.

With one hand I kept the lid raised while I peered into the bin's blue plastic depths. I wanted it to contain something I could recognize as the source of the putrid odour that had assaulted my nostrils as soon as I'd climbed the front steps. The bin contained nothing. It was empty. The air conditioner continued producing silence. I knew then that she was dead. The silence and the emptiness told me. The stench I refused to connect to her. I unlocked the door. The dog leash she'd fastened in lieu of a chain prevented the door from opening fully. I called out her name. I waited for her to answer. Being dead, she couldn't answer – I understood this but nonetheless called more loudly. I shouted a third time, then pulled the door shut, locked it, got on my bicycle, and pedalled home through the heat; and the people who passed me, in cars or on foot, were unaware that I no longer had the right to exist.

I asked my husband if he had a wire-snipping tool or something to cut through the chain preventing my sister's door from opening. He did not have a chain cutter, he said. She's killed herself, I replied, and the words made my body shake. I'm coming with you, he said. We arrived. I unlocked the door. He stuck his arm through the opening and unfastened the dog leash, just as I could have done had I thought to do so. The door swung fully open.

≈

Both in her bedroom in words on the wall, and in the kitchen, applying paint to canvas, she was addressing herself, or her many selves, of varying ages and genders. YOU CAN SAY GOODBYE, one or more reassured the others. You are allowed to leave.

She may also have been addressing me – the sister bound to find her body. Apart from her, only I had a key to the house. When convinced her words are aimed at me, I feel the blade of her anger twist. Directed at me, YOU CAN SAY GOODBYE becomes a command.

But in her careful penmanship, as she spells out her three reasons for putting a noose around her neck, I see no visible anger. Her handwriting appears calm. She has arrived at a decision. The power to act is hers, and this power has quieted her rage. She has decided that death is her best choice, her most potent means of self-expression.

Because of schizophrenia
Because of The Juniper Tree
Because of losing the house

She could have added: *Because of my fucking sister*. But she didn't. Though that is what I'm tempted to read in her third reason for leaving.

Christina wanted to stay on, in the house of our childhood – 'to do battle with the house,' she told her psychiatrist. She'd returned to the house four years earlier, when our mother, at the age of ninety-six, had moved to an institution for the elderly, and the house had become empty, not of possessions but of people. It was crammed full of art, furniture, books, memories.

≈

On a corner lot, a grey stucco house with gabled windows and protruding alcoves. At the front, a sitting room. Its teal-tiled fireplace drew well, never belched smoke, and when we were small, only in that sunniest room with its pale yellow carpet, pale sofa, pale curtains, and mahogany furniture passed down through our mother's family – in that room only, on whose wall hung the gilded mirror in which our great-great-grandfather had examined his reflection after being released from Libby Prison in an exchange of captives during the American Civil War – were we not allowed to leave our clothes, books, papers, toys, spoons, hairbrushes, cups, scissors, and other random objects strewn about, covering every surface. In the middle of the house, a dark dining room, and off it, on the street side, a small, bright kitchen with a window to the right of the stove, and to the left of the china cupboard a door heavily bolted, and behind this door three steps descending to a landing, where, from curiosity to see what was inside or from an actual need to sweep something up, something fallen and broken, we could open a shallow broom closet by pulling on two spherical red knobs attached to its two white doors, or having no need to sweep anything up, we could turn our backs on the broom closet and unhook the little chain securing the square door of the milk box, whose back was a second door that opened to the outside world. Inside this milk box, when we were small, our mother would leave a list for the milkman. And when it wasn't Christina's turn to tick the boxes beside the items our mother wanted, then it was my turn to excitedly pencil a mark where our mother's finger pointed, and a sudden importance and authority would hum throughout my body, the body of a girl who'd just ordered two bottles of milk. From the landing, my sister and I, or anyone else who was inside the house, could leave the house through a side door, once two stiff bolts were slid to one side and yet another chain was unhooked, or rather than stepping outdoors, my sister and I (or anyone else in the house) could descend into the basement, examine the jars of nails, the saws and hammers and lathes and chisels and levels and lead weights and wrenches and screwdrivers loosely arranged on the work bench in the corner where our father kept his tools, or we could run our hands over the smooth flank of the big oil tank beside the furnace, or we could eye the hulking furnace from a safe distance, or we could pull our damp clothes from the washing machine's cork-screw belly and toss them into the dryer, or poke our fingers into the crumbling mortar between the stones of the base-ment wall, or we could climb the wooden stairs back up to the kitchen, slip into the tiny washroom, pee, clean our hands, run through the dining room into the book-lined backroom, and, each gripping her thick stick of sidewalk chalk, draw a hopscotch in the shape of a huge clown's head on the old brown carpet, and hop on one foot from mouth to nose, then land with one foot on either ear, while our father, looking up from his newspaper, cocked his right eyebrow in surprise and asked, 'Should children be allowed to draw on carpets?' To which our mother answered that she couldn't see why not, and then our father laughed loudly, and we continued our game.

≈

A grey stucco house on a corner lot lined with trees. A tranquil neighbourhood of privilege and bucolic charm, wooden gates at either end to prevent the city's rush from encroaching. A road looped in the shape of an eight, enclosing a community tennis court, a ravine, a pond where koi fish swam, ducks floated, and turtles sunned on logs, Taddle Creek surfacing from under the city to feed the pond, then exit the wealthy, white enclave, vanishing once more beneath the paved metropolis. From this enclosed neighbourhood my sister yearned to leave, and much later refused to leave, unless on her own terms, that is to say, dead.

≈

Guilt distorts. Out of guilt I am thrusting into first place my sister's third reason to die: *Because of losing the house.*

She placed it last on her list. But does a final reason not function as a finger on the trigger? Though she did not use a gun.

A year after our mother died, I arrived at a decision, pressed to do so by lawyers. Urged to lay down a clear path forward by determining precisely how to carry out our mother's final wish, as stated in her will, that all she possessed be equally divided between her two daughters, and wanting my share, I concluded that the house should be sold, in a year, or two, or three, or two, or one, and that the proceeds be placed in a trust to support Christina. My decision, when I presented it to my sister, was not immutable. I gave a letter to her, to read with her psychiatrist – a letter I'd written, erased, and rewritten over a period of weeks of frantic self-inquiry. It ended by stating my willingness to discuss my decision, and hours after delivering it I slipped several postcards under her door, explaining that I planned to leave the city for a period of days but could cancel my trip if she wanted to speak with me after reading the letter, though I suspected I'd not be the person she'd want to speak with, not right away, and that I wanted her to know that already I was questioning the contents of the letter, and that perhaps the house needn't be sold in a year's time, as that seemed unnecessarily rushed.

Christina had asked that all discussion of our mother's estate occur in the presence of her psychiatrist. My letter was to prepare them, and to be followed by the three of us meeting in person, as we'd done in the past when an issue of contention had to be resolved.

A fraught event had occurred within weeks of our mother's death. My sister had asked me to help remove, from an upstairs room, a large, rolled-up carpet. It had become a breeding ground for moths. She'd refrained from asking for help while our mother was dying, since my hands were full, she said. But now the moths were so numerous, flitting about in every room, and she could not crush them on the walls fast enough to keep their numbers down, and her attempt at stifling them by wrapping a small duvet around one end of the carpet, which resembled a giant cigar, had failed.

Once we'd carried the giant cigar of a carpet outdoors and abandoned it on the back terrace, I'd proposed that I wash the small duvet in the machine in the basement. Since moving in, Christina had avoided the machine. Her dislike of basements made the sink in the bathroom off the kitchen a preferable place for cleaning clothes. If the one loose, long dress she wore all summer happened to need washing, she'd lift a portion of its cloth into the sink, without undressing, so that the rest of the garment continued to conceal her body, which she reviled, she told me, and did not want to lay eyes on.

One heavy dark blue dress for winter, and for summer a lighter one. Over either, she'd sometimes drape, always with style, more delicate fabrics with textures that pleased her, in contrasting shades of blue or grey. She had an impeccable sense of design. These additions she secured by means of safety pins arranged to climb her thigh in an elegant curve, or to cross her chest in an arabesque.

Always she held herself erect and appeared to glide down the sidewalk, a large-brimmed hat shading her face in every season. The studied rhythm of her steps and the ample flow of her garments disguised the awkwardness her medication-bloated body imposed on her.

As I opened the basement door she asked why I could not take the duvet home and use my own machine. I'd rather not, I said. There's a perfectly good one here. It was unlikely, I thought to myself, that the moth infestation would spread to my house were I to take the duvet home. Yet I insisted on using our mother's machine. I wanted, and stubbornly, to deal with the duvet there, in the house where it belonged. Perhaps my insistence sprang from a desire to demonstrate that cleaning could occur in the house. Christina had not allowed any substantial cleaning since moving in, three years earlier.

Within days of my using our mother's machine, a drain in the basement floor backed up, and my sister had to mop up quantities of fouled water. She asked that I call a plumber. I did so. It was odd, she remarked, that a drain should back up right after I'd used the washing machine. Perhaps the two events were related? She was right, I'd learn from the plumber. I'd shifted the position of a hose, which looked as if it might empty on the floor. Me poking the hose into the drain had caused the backup. But this she would never learn.

Whenever a repairperson was to come, Christina would leave the house first thing in the morning, and I would cycle over to let them in once they'd called or texted me to say they were on their way. To ensure she would not encounter the repairperson, Christina would refrain from returning until late in the afternoon. She'd force herself to stay out in the world hours longer than she could normally tolerate. The strain of such extended exposure to humans outside her house was worth it, she said, to avoid all possibility of meeting a stranger inside her home.

While work was being done, I'd wait in the front room. Eventually I'd sign any necessary papers, show the repairperson out, leave my sister a note conveying whatever information I'd received, lock the door behind me, and cycle home.

This time the repairperson, a plumber, arrived late, and so, though the trouble with the drain proved simple to fix, I was still in the front room writing Christina a note when she opened the door. Her face revealed surprise and irritation at finding me there. Ideally, by her own admission, she would have allowed nobody but herself to enter her home at any time and under any circumstances. But to me she could not deny entry since she needed me, and since the house belonged as much to me as to her. I asked if she wanted to hear the plumber's explanation. No, she said, no, she'd rather not. This angered me. Much of my day had been taken up with the plumber. It was her drain he'd come to fix, and my having caused the problem by wrongly repositioning a hose was a piece of information I decided to withhold, to refuse her the satisfaction of knowing that she'd been right in not wanting me to use our mother's old machine, she, my brilliant sister, who was so often right. I snapped at her that I'd leave my note on the front porch and go. No, she said, with great self-control, she was willing to listen, if I'd allow her first to get a drink of cold water, as it was horribly hot out, and she'd just walked from the bus stop. Of course, I agreed, she was most welcome to have a drink, and even to take her time. The plumber's news was good, and I'd relay it once she was ready.

A few weeks later, Christina e-mailed me to ask if I'd meet with her and her psychiatrist. We agreed on a day and time. I arrived at Dr. R's office expecting to discuss our mother's will. But the purpose of the meeting was to figure out how, the next time I let in a repairperson, I could inform Christina in advance of her return that the work was completed and I was leaving, so she could come home, certain I'd be gone by the time she got there. She did not want to experience again the shock of finding me in the house. Having to converse with me right when she'd been out in the world for an extended time, and tiredness was making her less able to cope with people, was what she wanted to avoid, for both our sakes. Also, could I please limit myself to completing the task she'd asked me to perform and not insist on doing something additional next time she was forced to turn to me for help? I'd recently insisted on washing a duvet. If I'd done so for an excuse to linger in the house, then she could arrange other times for me to come when she was not home. Yes, I agreed, I could limit myself to whatever task she requested, and, if a repairperson was needed, I could e-mail her from my phone once they'd done their work and I was departing. Since she did not have a phone, she could retrieve my message from a public computer at a municipal library, then return home without risk of encountering me. Would this resolve matters?

Dr. R asked my sister what she thought of my offer. Christina nodded her head in acceptance, then repeated her proposition, that if I wanted to spend more time in the house, dates could be arranged.

Less than a month had passed since our mother's death, and my days were now consumed with filling out forms, making phone calls, searching for requested documents, and meeting with lawyers.

Very soon a gathering was to take place in a gallery space: the one-hundredth-birthday party I'd planned for our mother before her death. I'd not cancelled the celebration. Many people would be coming, far too many for Christina to bear being present. That she couldn't attend did not bother her, she said. She'd hung one of our mother's old nightgowns from a hanger in the kitchen, and this made our mother present for her. In this private way she was marking our mother's passing. What she described moved me deeply. Often Christina's solutions were simple and powerful.

But her sudden suggestion, in Dr. R's office, that she might allow me a few hours in the house of my childhood at pre-arranged times shot through me like an arrow, and I stated that I did not want to 'linger,' that the house felt creepy and I did not want to be in it.

Christina started to shake. Her arms trembled, and her legs too. 'I never knew,' she cried out, 'that you found the way I live "creepy." I know there are lots of people who find art made by schizophrenics "creepy," but you've never used that word about my art, you've never told me that you hate how I live.'

The word *creepy* had slipped from me, in my fury at her wanting to increasingly control my entries and exits from our childhood home, which she'd temporarily returned to, then incrementally made her own. I'd not intended to insult her way of living. But I had knowingly wanted to be violent, to free myself from her control by rejecting the house, by declaring that I had no desire to 'linger' within it.

That she felt controlled by me, imprisoned in her dependence on my aid, did not lessen the degree to which I felt at risk of being controlled by her. 'It's not your art I find disturbing,' I said. 'It's not everything about the way you live that makes me uncomfortable in the house. But I need air, and light, and you need to keep both those things out. So the windows are all closed and the curtains drawn, and – '

Her psychiatrist interjected: 'She can't hear you. She's too upset. What you said to her was very hurtful.' But

Christina's shaking had diminished, and I asked her if my explanation was helping, and I repeated my apology. Yes, she told me, my words helped – a bit. Minutes later I was asked to leave, so Christina and her psychiatrist could spend what remained of their session in private.

Released, I sat on the sidewalk beside my locked bicycle, unable to summon the energy to ride home.

Late that night, I woke in bed and knew that part of what had unravelled me was the three-way tugging of a triangle formed by Christina, her psychiatrist, and me. This present triangle potently evoked a past one formed by Christina, our mother, and me. From that earlier geometry I vividly recalled our mother's propensity to defend her fragile eldest from her less sensitive younger daughter. She'd also defended her eldest from our critical father, and from the world as a whole. Realizing that Dr. R's reprimand – her telling me how hurtful my word *creepy* was – had replicated, or resurrected in my ear, our mother's quick correcting of anyone whose words caused Christina visible distress, I understood why exhaustion had swallowed me as I left Dr. R's office.

Lying on my back in my bed, in the dark, I promised myself that the next time my sister and her psychiatrist asked me to meet with them, I'd request permission to bring a trusted friend – I'd make sure that the encounter took the shape of a square or a circle, anything but a triangle.

The following week, Christina asked me to come over to the house. She'd opened the curtains of one window in the front room, had cleared the surface of a table in front of the newly light-filled window, and had placed a chair for me to sit on. 'This way,' she told me, 'the next time you come over to wait for a repairman, you'll be more comfortable.'

Her generosity made me want to weep. She'd thought over the reasons I'd given for not liking to be in the house and had accommodated me. She'd moved her art, any of it that had been in the front room, into different rooms. With true care she'd created a place in the house where I might feel at ease. Her gesture felt loving and therefore confusing. I'd learned to be always on my guard, to expect retaliation at any moment, as she was easily alarmed, often inhabited by rage, and frequently felt attacked when no attack was intended. I expect she'd have said the same of me – that my retaliations came at her without warning.

The chair Christina placed in front of the table in front of the light-filled window – when I picture, now, that inviting arrangement of chair, table, and window, my fingers stop typing, my breath catches, and an ache forms in my chest.

≈

Property – from *proprietās*, 'something personal' in Latin, and from *proprius*, 'one's own.'

own – 1. a. (intensifier): *John's own idea.* b. (as *pron.*): *I'll use my own.* 2. on behalf of oneself or in relation to oneself: *he is his own worst enemy.* 3. come into one's own. a. to fulfill one's potential. b. to receive what is due to one. 4. hold one's own. to maintain one's situation or position, esp. in spite of opposition or difficulty. 5. on one's own. a. without help. b. by oneself; alone. ~*vb.* 6. (*tr.*) to have as one's possession. 7. (when *intr.*, often foll. by *up*, *to*, or *up to*) to confess or admit; acknowledge ... [OE *āgen*, orig. p.p. of *āgan* to have. See OWE]

owe – 1. to be under the obligation to pay (someone) to the amount of. 2. (*intr.*) to be in debt: *he still owes for his house.* 3. (often foll. by *to*) to have as a result (of). 4. to feel the need or obligation to do, give, etc. ... [OE *āgan*: to have (C12: to have to)]

The Old English *āgan* makes sister-words of *own* and *owe*.

≈

Half a year or so before our mother's death, Dr. R learned from Christina that I was taking our mother for radiation treatments twice a week to slow the progress of a skin cancer that had manifested in her cheek, then attached itself to her jawbone. Dr. R insisted that Christina invite me to one of their weekly therapy sessions, so the three of us could discuss where Christina was to live in her imminently motherless future.

Once we were all seated, Dr. R asked who would like to speak first. I suggested that Christina begin. Straight away she warned me: 'If I'm forced to leave the house as soon as Mom dies, you'll just find a body.' I promised her that what she was describing would not happen. Nothing would unfold quickly. There would be a lot to sort out. It would take at least a year, and I hoped she'd be able to stay in the house until she turned sixty-five, at which time I'd help her to move into an apartment, possibly in the building for the elderly where our mother was now living. It was a pleasant place, already familiar to her, in a neighbourhood she knew well, and many of its residents lived in complete independence. She'd only have to share the elevator with older people, who she might find less threatening than those she'd ride enclosed with, up and down, in a regular building. Furthermore, by making this move now, she'd not have to move again as she herself aged.

When asked by Dr. R what she thought of my proposal, Christina murmured that it sounded 'okay.' But once I'd left the room, she told her psychiatrist that my plan to semi-institutionalize her when she turned sixty-five made no difference, as she had no intention of living that long.

What she said in my absence – about planning to die before she reached sixty-five – I would not learn until after her suicide.

≈

Our mother died. Christina made clear that she did not want to leave the house and felt she had a right to stay there, and believed that I should find a way to make this possible.

In her voice I heard determination, a desire to impose her will on me. Her threat to kill herself resurfaced in my mind and hardened me. Her promise of suicide, were her needs not met, strengthened my inclination to resist her demands. I would have blood on my hands if I did not give her what she wanted – what I perceived to be blackmail deafened me. More loudly than I heard the true need she was expressing, I heard threat, and a will to punish if she was not obeyed. My own desires and fears determined what I heard in her words. Besides anger and threat, her words contained fear. But if I allowed myself to feel her fear, her vulnerability would become too real, and I, not wanting her to come to any harm, would become her prisoner – unable to refuse her anything, which her fear dictated I should provide. And her fears were limitless. No, the limitless nature of her demands was my invention, my own fear speaking. I feared her will, her authority within me. She asked only to be permitted to keep inhabiting deeply familiar rooms. No, she did not ask, she required.

≈

She'd stopped taking her medications, she'd told me, earlier that month. In what month? May? Or not until June of that year? Of the physical side effects she'd been speaking for some time – they were worsening, proving unbearable: bloated belly, bleeding anus, weight gain, trouble sleeping, trouble staying awake, and the muscles of her jaw locking when she tried to speak.

She'd stopped her medications against the advice of Dr. R, who would have preferred she change drugs to lessen the side effects, rather than take no drugs at all.

Unmedicated, she immediately felt more alive, more herself. The internal voices were numerous and strong, but she had ways of dealing with them, she assured me. We met at the Gardiner Museum to see the Ai Weiwei exhibit. It was the first time in years that we'd visited a gallery together.

As we walked in a circle around an immense and ancient ceramic jar, upon which Ai Weiwei had inscribed 'Coca Cola' in red pigment, collapsing history while commenting on its commodification, I and maybe she didn't know that in a matter of months she'd kill herself.

Upon leaving the gallery, we went into the museum's restaurant. The restaurant, she said, didn't frighten her – its spaciousness and small number of customers compensating for its lack of familiarity. We sat down, ordered coffee and scones.

Two years earlier, we'd begun writing a book together, a work of call and response about her relationship to language and mine. She'd asked that her words occupy always the left page and mine the opposite page to prevent contamination in either direction. But as our project progressed, she'd started typing footnotes on some of my pages.

She used a manual typewriter, I used a word processor. We kept our work in a ring binder to which I added my printed-out responses to whatever texts she'd introduced the last time the binder was in her hands. The red plastic binder travelled back and forth between us. Her footnotes appearing on my pages suggested to me that her need for distance was lessening, her trust expanding, and soon, as if to confirm this, she would begin composing letters to me several pages long to be included in our book.

Now our collaboration was to be published. In mid-September, printed and bound, it would enter the wider world.

She'd composed a speech, which she hoped someone might read at the launch of *Sister Language*. From her voluminous book bag, her 'lug bag,' she extracted two tightly typed pages and handed them across the table to me to read. In her speech, she thanked me for my part in creating our book and stated that the *Sister Language* experience had 'rescued' her 'from hell.'

'My creative and intellectual vigour – and my selfhood – have been restored. The *Sister Language* experience has worked, it has reached me and strengthened me.'

Her speech was a declaration of freedom, banged out on her manual typewriter. In each word I could hear the sound and force of metal keys striking an inked ribbon, of tiny hammers propelled downward by the energy of her mind travelling through her fingers.

Sister Language had 'not only achieved what ten years of dedicated professional psychiatric treatment failed to achieve,' it had 'begun to reverse some of the corrosive and erosive effects of that well-intentioned but ultimately, for me, disastrous treatment.'

As I read her carefully constructed statement, fear and excitement danced inside me. I looked up from her typed words into her face, into her discerning blue eyes. 'With you as my ally, I don't need Dr. R anymore,' she said.

≈

Scared that she would leave her psychiatrist and that I alone would be faced with assisting her in orchestrating her volatile energies, and knowing that we'd not yet resolved what was to be done about the house, one afternoon I knocked on her door. If she was home and let me in, I intended to advise her to stick with Dr. R, at least until our mother's will was settled.

In the front room we argued. She stated her reasons for wanting to stay in the house and said that she could not understand why I was not happy to do as she asked. Why did I insist on holding on to my full share, the rural lands, which exceeded my needs, when by sacrificing a portion of what I was to receive I could enable her to stay in the house indefinitely, and I'd be rich from the sale of land and could be perfectly happy. I questioned her math. She told me that my math did not interest her, she'd done her own. Quickly the argument veered from property to autonomy and our respective right to each define her own happiness, and soon she shouted at me to leave. A few days later we met again, in the hallway of the house, and spoke briefly about our book. A photo of her painting *White on White* was to be included and the colour fuchsia removed from the cover, as she'd requested.

We would never again stand in each other's presence and speak.

Never again – death's finality is like a blow to the head. Were life a cartoon, being punched by the death of a person you love would make you see stars.

After our hallway conversation, I delivered my letter; next I slipped my self-questioning postcards under her door. She responded with an e-mail, asking that we forgo any meetings in person for the time being. She needed space. She and Dr. R were trying to keep her stable until the book launch. Our argument in the front room had left her distraught. She thanked me for *Sister Language*. Would I, please, not contact her.

I wanted to go to her then and tell her to ignore my letter and postcards, tell her that I loved her, and that I was prepared to do whatever was necessary to keep her safe in the house for as long as possible, though I could not promise how long that would be. But I'd been advised that my duty was to be clear, to present my arguments, then stand by them. I decided it was best to give Christina and Dr. R time to prepare a carefully considered response to my letter before I allowed myself to start retracting my words. It was important, I'd been warned, that I not offer to alter my decisions unless I had a new and clear path forward worked out, one I was sure I could live with.

I'd been to see my doctor and had asked her to refer me to a psychiatrist. I wanted someone to help me weigh my sister's threat to kill herself and assist me in sorting out my feelings, so I could arrive at a decision about the house. My doctor refused to refer me. 'You are strong,' she said. 'You can figure out what you want and what you think is best. Your sister isn't going to kill herself. What she requires from you is a clear decision. If she's schizophrenic, the one thing you can be sure of is that she's only able to think about herself and her needs, not yours. So, you must decide what is best for you.'

I don't hold my doctor responsible for my actions, or for my sister's death. Neither do I thank her for speaking with authority about my sister when she lacked the knowledge to do so, and for refusing to direct me to a psychiatrist. After Christina's suicide I went to see my doctor again. Lack of sleep was corroding my ability to function. I told her that her prediction had proven wrong. I told her that my sister would still be alive were it not for the decisions I'd taken. She answered that since the advice she'd given me had proven misleading, I should conclude that any wrongdoing that had occurred had not all been caused by me. My decisions had not been entirely mine, influenced as I'd been by others. She did not expect I'd keep blaming myself for long, she said, since I was not narcissistic enough to keep doing so. I responded by repeating my need for something to help me sleep at night.

≈

When does a desire become a need? When you cannot live without it. What if a person is willing to kill themself because they cannot have what they want? Our mother's properties were to be divided evenly between her two daughters. But life had not treated her two daughters even-handedly. How could I consider moving a paranoid person out of a fully detached house, her childhood home, into an apartment, likely thin-walled, knowing that every sound from behind a shared wall could induce psychosis, I ask myself, and the first answer is short and condemns me tidily: selfishness. But the second answer to form in my mind, and innards, is long. When I tug on it, the roots of my resistance are revealed; the many hidden roots of my actions during the final months of our sisterhood branch out and dangle.

≈

Guilt makes me the eye of her storm; it places me at the centre of her story and attributes resolve to my actions, a resolve that is a lie. My guilt is not a lie. I cling to it. Guilt protects me from grief. If I allow my attention to detach from my role in her death, if I allow my mind to focus on her suffering instead of my guilt, then her pain rises to my waist, my armpits, my neck.

≈

In childhood, on our road's steep descent toward the lower gates, often my sister and I would fall from our bicycles, scraping our knees. Most of the dangers we dodged were imaginary, monstrous. On the winter pond we learned to skate, pushing folding kitchen chairs across the ice to keep our balance. Giant oak trees cast their cooling shade over our summer games. Indoors, where walls and ceiling met, the aged plaster curved, giving to each room a tenderness. Floors creaked, doorways sloped, radiators throbbed and clanked. My sister and I were each handed a cup and allowed to tend the radiators. We'd turn the knob that released trapped air from hot pipes. The air escaped, and next came drops of stale water, a few to be caught in her cup and a few in mine, then we tightened the knob that closed the valve. How powerful we felt, or I did, tending the radiators. What my sister felt I did not ask, certain as I was that her emotions corresponded to mine. I was a young child and believed that everyone felt as I did.

≈

We locate ourselves in our bodies, on the land, in the rooms we inhabit, and in the languages we speak. Body, land, room, and language provide the psyche with a home.

Because of schizophrenia, said Christina, locating herself was a chronic challenge, an often insurmountable feat. Only in language did she truly exist – so she insisted. Her home was a proliferation of neologisms, an ever-expanding universe of words decomposing and recomposing. Her mind eschewed fixity of language and prescribed syntax. In nothing fixed or prescribed could she be at home.

Her body she increasingly reviled. In her forties and fifties its sexual desires threatened her. Later, its medication-induced bloating disgusted her. As she turned sixty, its signs of deterioration frightened her. She labelled her body a 'sack of putrefaction.'

The texts she typed she archived in binders, and the binders became additional rooms in the house, she told me. She did not have to reread what she'd written to know that those rooms existed, and that she could enter or leave them at will.

≈

In summer we counted the days until the month of August freed our father from his work; then the four of us, towing a wooden boat behind our car, left the city. The boat was painted gleaming white. It belonged to our uncle Pete, from whom our father rented it each year. It could speed through water, as if pulled by thirty-nine horses – so promised the outboard motor at its stern. Our father would raise his foot to brace himself, pull and pull on the motor's cord, and if the engine failed to turn over, if none of the horses neighed, he'd curse and go at it again.

On a wooden deck, on an island of rock, where pine trees grew from pockets of soil and slapping water had smoothed the shore over millennia, we stood side by side, two small naked sisters, and used our fingers to aim our urine in an outward arc across moss and fallen leaves, competing to see who could strike the farthest with her pee.

The deck spanned the width of the cottage, which had neither electricity nor plumbing and overlooked the wide mouth of a bay. In the woods our father had dug a pit, cut a slender cedar tree, stripped it of its bark, planed it smooth, nailed it horizontally to two live pines, and on this bar he'd fashioned, we'd perch to defecate in the pit. He'd proposed to build an outhouse, but our mother had declined the idea of an odour-enclosing structure, and so he'd made a single wall from salvaged planks to block the pit from view; no roof protected us from rain, and from our open perch we could see through the forest down to the lake. From the lake we carried water in buckets for cooking, drinking, and washing. The cottage sat on pillars, its floor a single layer of plywood supported by thick beams. When we walked, our feet made a hollow sound. Two tanks of propane under the floor fed a stove in the kitchen, a small refrigerator (recycled from a New York apartment), and a single light by which our parents read to us at night, our four folding chairs squeezed into the narrow bright space, darkness consuming the rest of the cottage. When lightning cracked and thunder rolled, reverberating off cliffs, the wall of glass windows facing the water rattled, and our parents hurried out and down through the woods to the lake to better secure the motorboat, which our father worried might be swept onto the rocks. Any damage to the hull would release the wrath of his older brother, a wrath he feared, though not so intensely as he feared his own guilt, which could dash him on the rocks for failing to protect his brother's property from destruction.

≈

On many nights since my sister's suicide, since she tumbled herself out of bed with a noose around her neck, the noose secured to the bedpost, I've tumbled back through time and landed in my bed on the island of our childhood:

We both are small. In the rain-lashed window above our heads, towering pines bend in a flash of white light followed by thunder. I pull my arm from under the covers, reach into the abyss separating my bed from Christina's, whisper 'I'm scared,' and straight away her arm appears. Her hand holds mine. Quietly we speak, quietly so as not to disturb the dark. Her words, and her fingers intertwined with mine, erase my fears, and through the woods our parents come, the faint beams of their flashlights illuminating their return.

2

In adulthood we stopped speaking of childhood. The past became a forbidden subject. We exchanged no memories.

She gave, as her second reason to die, the title of a fairy tale with no fairies in it. *Because of The Juniper Tree*. I am ending my life because of a tale by the Brothers Grimm, in which a boy is murdered by his stepmother and fed to his oblivious father.

The boy asks his stepmother if he may take an apple from the wooden chest open in front of him. 'Yes,' she answers. 'Go ahead. Reach in and choose the reddest.' The boy bends over to get a better look. Down comes the lid, severing the boy's head from his body. Next the stepmother sits him upright on a chair, puts an apple in his lap, and balances his head on his neck. Around his neck she ties a red handkerchief. Soon the boy's little sister comes home. She sees her brother's apple and asks, 'Can I have one?' 'Tell your brother to give you his,' answers the stepmother. The girl does as she's told. She asks her brother, but he ignores her. Mute, immobile, he stares straight ahead. 'He wouldn't give it to me,' she complains. 'Ask him again,' the stepmother instructs. 'If he says nothing, slap him on the cheek for his rudeness.' A second time the girl asks her brother for his apple. He ignores her. She slaps his cheek. His head falls to the floor and rolls. Horrified, the little girl runs from the room. The stepmother shouts after her: 'What have you done? Look! You've killed your brother.' The stepmother chops the boy into pieces and cooks him in a pot. Soon her husband comes home. She ladles the steaming stew onto his plate. He eats it all and asks for more. The little girl leaves her food untouched. The father asks his wife, 'Where is my son?' She answers that the boy has gone to a nearby village on an errand. The father continues eating. Each small bone he gnaws clean he tosses under the table. The sister slips to the floor and gathers the bones in her napkin. In the garden she plants them. A juniper tree grows. A bird lands on its uppermost branch. The bird surveys the countryside, then flies away. It finds a millstone and carries it through the air, looking for the stepmother. A great weight falls from the sky. It crushes the wicked woman into the ground. Freed from evil, the boy steps out of the juniper tree.

Because of The Juniper Tree – by this Christina meant that her second reason for dying was to escape the horror of having been killed by her mother and fed to her father.

Christina knew I was familiar with 'The Juniper Tree,' which I'd inserted in one of my novels, *The Incident Report*. What drew me to the tale, I'd told her, was how it laid bare human deviousness, the slipperiness of blame, the vulnerability of children to adult manipulation.

Our human adeptness at shaping narrative to suit our needs has fascinated me for as long as I can remember. When I mentioned the vulnerability of children to my sister, it was all children I had in mind. But in my attraction to 'The Juniper Tree,' Christina saw evidence that I had witnessed, as a child, monstrous acts of abuse of which she'd been the victim.

All I wrote and said she probed for clues to support a vision of the past she believed in but could not locate in memory. Trauma, explosive as a dying star, can create a void. Illness can produce delusion. Within Christina, trauma, or delusion, or both, were at work.

As folktales make clear, we all live in danger of being eaten by those closest to us. To engage with others is to risk having your soul and psyche consumed by another.

≈

In his novel *When We Cease to Understand the World*, Benjamín Labatut reimagines the terror experienced by German astrophysicist Karl Schwarzschild in 1915, when his calculations pointed to the existence of black holes in space:

> If matter were prone to birthing monsters of this kind, Schwarzschild asked with a trembling voice, were there correlations with the human psyche? Could a sufficient concentration of human will ... unleash something comparable ... Schwarzschild was inconsolable. He babbled about a black sun dawning over the horizon, capable of engulfing the entire world ...

Schwartzchild would die of illness in 1916, while serving in the German army. He'd not witness the black dawn of Nazism, or of the nuclear bomb, or of climate change. But he knew that the world was vulnerable to being swallowed whole.

> [T]here existed a limit, a barrier that marked a point of no return. After crossing that line, any object – from a whole planet to a minuscule subatomic particle – would be trapped forever.

Reading about black holes, I'm tempted to picture my sister being pulled by illness over a line of no return. Possibly a misplaced desire to separate illness from health, to draw a clear boundary between them, fuels my imagination. Or I want there to have been a moment when a force as powerful as physics or fate made her journey irreversible because the existence of such a decisive moment would relieve me of all responsibility for having failed to coax her back to this side of what I'm now conceiving to have been a Schwarzschild radius.

≈

'Have I gone mad because my parents were Nazis, or do I believe they were Nazis because I am mad? At least I can still ask this question' – Christina wrote in one of many journals she kept in her fifties.

To her question – were our parents Nazis? – I have an answer. But it is my answer, not hers.

≈

Her second-to-last home was a semi-detached house that she quickly came to loathe, convinced that every sound made by her neighbour (with whom she shared a wall) was a calculated response to a sound she'd made, his goal being to undermine her sanity through covert communication.

On the walls of each room in that house, upstairs and down, she'd painted declarations in letters four inches tall, or taller.

'Never tell' 'There is nothing' 'Hello there' 'It can't (sic) be bandaged it won't heal' 'The virgin is no harlot' 'The punishment for profligacy is death' 'Meet with surveillance teem' 'Live or die?' 'I just want to die/there will be no blood/everything is lace' 'Make no mention.'

The purpose of these declarations she outlined in her journal:

HUMANS OH HUMANS do you know about my walls? These are some of the messages I've painted in Iron Oxide Red or Mars/Ivory black on the walls that by virtue of these messages are more mine and less YOURS YOU HUMANS.

≈

The small semi-detached brick house, Christina's second-to-last home, perched on a rise of land, could be reached only by climbing a steep set of concrete stairs. On the day she and I first visited the place, to assess its suitability as a possible home for her, I spoke enthusiastically of its elevated location. From her high front porch she would be able to look down on the street and observe passersby from a safe distance.

She agreed that the steep stairs pleased her, and gave her own reason for their appeal: 'They'll be too difficult for Mom to climb, so she won't be able to come in.'

The very person providing Christina with a new home, a place of her own, my sister was most eager to keep out.

That Christina depended on our mother for her material well-being increased her distrust and her resentment of her. The more Christina depended on someone, the more inclined she was to resent and distrust them. She felt gratitude. But being helped made her beholden. Whoever she most depended upon was best positioned to take control of her.

'I trust no one,' Christina would often remind me. 'It's not just you, but everyone.'

≈

But I've moved forward too quickly in my telling of Christina's story, which differs greatly from the one she'd tell, and differs also from the story I told a year ago, which differed from the one I told two years earlier. Ever since her death, I've been writing, erasing, and rewriting this disobedient tale.

I want to return to the basement apartment from which she escaped to the semi-detached house perched on a rise. I want to go back and have a closer look at that tiny apartment I found for her in a hurry, needing to remove her quickly from our mother's house, where she'd just attempted suicide.

She'd returned from Victoria, where for twenty years she'd lived enclosed in the safety of a nearly sexless marriage to a young man who adored her, whom she'd met in her twenties and loved, but not with her body, not fully, and had finally worked up her courage to leave, since it was women she desired.

She'd returned to Toronto, hoping, she told me, to find anonymity, here, in the city of her childhood and adolescence, where, yes, she would risk encountering her past at every corner, but the lesbian scene might be less incestuous, and the city's size would allow her to go unnoticed no matter how unconventional her appearance. In Victoria she'd begun painting Basquiat-like heads on the jackets she wore, and admiring tourists would approach her on the street, asking to take her photo. In Toronto she hoped to wander unseen from one bookstore to the next, and in and out of art galleries and cafés.

The basement apartment, when I first went to see it, looked clean. It was situated on a quiet, tree-lined side street, in a neighbourhood Christina liked. A short walk away were grocery stores, cafés, a bookshop, a pharmacy. What's more, the apartment's owner was a woman, an acquaintance of mine who I felt I could trust, and someone Christina might find less threatening than a male landlord. I considered it a stroke of luck that such a suitable apartment had come available right when Christina, by trying to kill herself, had made it clear she could not continue living under the same roof as our mother, who'd taken her in when she arrived from Victoria, jobless and homeless.

Once settled into her apartment, she cut off all communication with our mother. She and I continued to meet in various cafés until, one afternoon, I handed her a note that our mother had asked me to deliver. Then she severed all ties with me too.

Five years of silence followed, until a centipede infestation compelled her to contact our mother. Without financial help she could not escape her basement apartment, which was overrun. In response to her landlord's refusal to recognize the infestation as real, she'd taken to leaving crushed centipedes on the walls as evidence. She showed me many tiny corpses distributed across the white expanse above her sofa. Silent and speedy, materializing out of nowhere on their multiple legs, centipedes were psychosis-inducing, she explained. Spring was when they hatched. If I could not find her somewhere centipede-free to live before the return of spring, she would not make it.

I tried to picture in what kind of apartment she might feel safe and had difficulty imagining her on the upper floor of a tall building. Riding in an elevator, she might suddenly suspect a fellow passenger of being her enemy. She collected scrap metal, wood, and abandoned objects on her long daily walks, and from these found materials produced powerful art. I pictured her distraught, squeezed into a crowded elevator, her odd treasures from the street protruding from under her arms. I pictured her lugging her materials across a lobby, headed for the stairwell, wanting to hurry out of sight but too weighed down. It would be best, I concluded, if she could live in a house, as this would give her direct and private access to the street.

If a house could be bought there'd be no landlord for Christina to deal with or for me to negotiate with on her behalf. I approached our mother to see what might be possible. Our mother expressed her willingness to invest her savings, if I could find an affordable house, organize the purchase, and maintain the property for however long my sister lived there. The house would be placed in a trust in Christina's name. I thanked our mother, informed Christina, and she and I began looking. We restricted ourselves to the part of the city in which I lived. It was an area Christina knew well, and for me it would be easier to take care of her new home if it were within walking distance of my own.

The most promising house we found was semi-detached and perched on a rise. Its basement wall had shifted in the past but the problem had been corrected, said the inspector's report.

Again I've moved forward too fast. I want to go back to the months Christina spent living with our mother, who so eagerly took her in when she returned from Victoria, months during which Christina appeared to thrive, spending her days reading, writing, reacquainting herself with the city, and exclaiming her relief at having escaped the claustrophobia of Victoria. Of her belief that our mother was engineering her mental collapse, she said nothing. Nor did she mention the antidepressant prescribed by her GP in Victoria, a medication she'd run out of and could no longer obtain.

In Toronto she had no doctor. Fear prevented her from applying for an Ontario health card, and this fear she hid. She hoped to delay, for as long as possible, having to engage with a government institution. All government institutions were octopus-like, with their many arms and surreptitious reach.

To enter a ServiceOntario reception centre, then wait in a chair for her number to be called, then present her identification papers to a stranger behind a wicket – a person empowered to assess her worthiness without knowing her – would have felt as terrifying as queuing in Dr. Mengele's Nazi waiting room. This she told me, later. How could she have waited calmly in line to be admitted into a secret laboratory run by sadists? She'd considered wearing dark glasses, headphones, and blasting her brain with punk rock to dull her awareness of the ServiceOntario reception centre, but still she could not bring herself to go there and apply for her health card. To sleep at night she took Gravol, a mild, over-the-counter medication for nausea, which our mother used to give us on long road trips when we were small and suffered from carsickness.

Her insomnia she did not hide from me. I too was a poor sleeper. Trouble sleeping she could count on me to understand.

She felt unsure, she said, how to go about making new friends and was reluctant to connect with old ones from her high school years. I set about introducing her to friends of mine.

One weekend, I took my mother to her cabin in the countryside for a change of scene. The lowering sun ignited the distant hills as I was clearing the dishes from an outdoor table and our mother was studying the sky and the horizon with her painter's eyes. My cellphone rang. 'Christina is in the hospital,' said a voice. Whose voice I don't remember.

≈

A successful painter, K, a friend of our mother's, well on in her eighties, had a live-in housekeeper, P, who often telephoned our mother to complain of K's impatience and dictatorial behaviour. Our mother would listen and offer sympathy, agreeing that K could be, at times, a difficult and demanding woman. Perhaps our mother, who envied the mark K had made in the Canadian art scene, experienced a perverse pleasure hearing K being maligned by her housekeeper.

Our mother admired K's work and felt a reluctant affection for K, who gave our mother's work intermittent attention and readily agreed that our mother deserved far more public recognition than she'd so far received. Often the two of them went out to dinner, or to galleries. They had friends in common.

The weekend I took our mother to the countryside, K's housekeeper, P, hoping for a sympathetic listener, phoned our mother's house in the city. But the voice that answered was not our mother's, and though the person on the other end of the line was trying to form words, they were failing, then the line went dead. P drove to our mother's house, rang the bell, knocked on the door, tugged at it, ran to the houses of neighbours, asking if anyone had a key.

Not long before the phone rang, Christina had been floating just below the kitchen ceiling, observing below her a separate version of herself who stood by the sink swallowing a fistful of pills.

The strength of Christina's heart, her ability to answer the phone when it rang and her impulse to do so, the chance timing of the call, and P's concern and quick actions – these combined elements resulted in my sister not dying. About this outcome my sister felt ambivalent, she said, as I pulled up a chair beside her hospital bed.

The day she was to be discharged from the hospital, a male psychiatrist entered her room and, wanting to rest his legs, chose her bed as a place to sit. Or perhaps he had some other reason for sitting down there, beside her, on her bed. Convinced by where he'd chosen to sit that he might also choose to rape her, said Christina, she answered 'Yes' when he enquired if she had a therapist lined up to attend her needs outside the hospital. 'I gave him the answer that would get him out of my room the fastest.' In truth she had no therapist. The psychiatrist responsible for releasing her back into the world did not ask for the name of the professional she claimed would be taking charge of guiding her toward stability. She was discharged with no plan in place for her to receive the care she required to continue surviving, let alone to mend.

Repeatedly I called the hospital to request outpatient assistance for my still-suicidal sister. My messages of distress inspired no response. Until one day the psychiatrist who'd sat on Christina's bed grew tired of my recorded voice (or of reports of my calls) and phoned me to ask if I knew the meaning of the word *confidentiality*. Yes, I assured him, I did. Well, he said, my behaviour suggested the opposite. He should not, he said, be speaking to me at all. My harassment of him and his staff must cease. The only person with whom he was willing to discuss my sister was my sister. That using a telephone terrified her, and that she refused to speak with him herself but had agreed I might call on her behalf, did not interest him. Confidentiality was crucial – this I agreed. But in his tone and words I heard no true concern for my sister's well-being, which confidentiality was intended to protect. He expressed no desire to address the predicament in which she and I found ourselves, given her wise unwillingness to communicate with him directly.

Christina agreed to come to my house to stay until I could find her a place of her own. Several weeks later, she moved into the furnished duplex of a friend of mine who'd gone abroad. There she could remain for up to a month at most. I started looking for an apartment she could rent for longer.

My friend's home was very pretty. Our mother, in conversation with Christina, referred to it as Christina's 'boutique hotel.' The term angered my sister. 'Hotel' implied vacation. But she was not on vacation, she was recovering from a failed attempt to kill herself.

'*Boutique hotel*,' Christina seethed. 'I asked Mom exactly what she meant, and she put on an air of innocence. She was just confirming that the place where I'm staying is the way I've described it: small but luxurious, too frilly for my taste. That's all she meant. Any biting meaning is all in my head. Her nastiness is my invention. She makes me feel crazy. She's always doing this to me. She denies her awareness so she can hurt me with impunity, and if her little game corrodes my faith in my ability to interpret reality, then that makes her all the stronger, and better equipped to undermine me.'

'Boutique hotel' = 'Boutique hotel.'

'Boutique hotel' = 'So, now you're too special and important to settle for a room in my house? The home of your childhood is no longer good enough for you?'

'Boutique hotel' = 'That pretty place, which you say you're grateful for but find too precious in its decor, well, I'm lightly mocking it in emulation of you, to show that I share your disdain for anything that doesn't fit your aesthetics.'

'Boutique hotel' = 'Does your need to escape my house in order to recover mean that what drove you to suicide was having to live under the same roof as me?'

Not having heard our mother's tone of voice, I could not decide how to translate 'boutique hotel.'

I could imagine our mother expressing hurt and resentment obliquely, feelings of shame preventing her from articulating her pain directly, given Christina's intense suffering, which so outweighed her own.

Our mother's indirections made her human, no more calculating or cruel than the next person.

Yet I could understand my sister's frustration.

Not infrequently, I too would confront our mother over something she'd said, and she'd claim innocence, expressing surprise at any unkind meaning her words could be understood to convey. Her denial of any awareness that her words might be interpreted in more ways than one added a thread of distrust to the weave of my connection to our mother.

But my reserve of trust was greater than Christina's.

I am writing these words, this paragraph, wearing an ochre scarf my mother bought in Paris nearly seventy years ago. Her scarf is made of softest silk. I wear it to draw my mother close to me. She possessed softness and gave of her softness. That she now and again shot a poisonous dart confused and angered Christina more than it did me.

Not only did Christina hunger for logic and consistency in all things, including humans, but she'd been made promises by our mother, so she felt – promises that our mother, over time, couldn't keep: of exclusivity, of an unflawed closeness, of a golden bond between them.

The love my mother felt for me differed from the love she felt for my sister. However devoted our mother was to me, my sister occupied a place more central in her heart. How did I learn this? From a look in her eye? From a change in tone when she addressed my sister? Or was it my nature to be jealous? Did a demon of envy inhabit me and tell me I'd been assigned second place? Demons like to tell stories. The darkness of the world enters us. So does the light. We are stories woven from darkness and light. Some of the darkness that slips within us we turn into light, and some of it we twist into a denser darkness that takes the shape of a demon voice inside us, urging us to produce more darkness.

There are many ways I can make sense of my jealousy. The story I'm telling here, about my sister's central place in my mother's heart, I've told so often it sounds true to me. But now that I return to it, rereading these sentences written several days ago, I hear my mother protest, with a quaver of surprise and pain, 'Oh, no. No. No. I loved you both. I loved you differently. You were such different daughters. But neither of you did I love more than the other. No. No.' And her eyes fill with sorrow.

≈

Our mother spent the 1940s in New York, painting mostly abstract works, many of great beauty.

She lived in one large room, she told me. It had a high ceiling, and big windows that let in good light. In this room stood an easel, a bed, a wardrobe, a table, two chairs, a hotplate, and an icebox. Once a week, or perhaps more frequently, an elderly man wearing a rubber cape would climb the steep stairs to her room. His cape prevented his burden – a large block of ice – from soaking his back.

Soot collected on her deep windowsill, and the sight of it saddened her. The loneliness of the city was finding its way into her room and accumulating as soot. Down the hall a shared bathroom. Below her room, a wine shop doing brisk business.

One evening, in a bar, a crashing sound made her turn. Jackson Pollock, felled by alcohol, hit the floor. The sight of him more repelled than excited her. She kept what she'd witnessed alive in her mind as proof that she did not desire to squeeze her way into that huddle of male painters – Kline, Motherwell, de Kooning, and Pollock – whose artistic daring was inspiring her but from whose public displays of freedom she recoiled; in any case, for none of them did she exist, though she had true talent, she'd been told, and told herself, yes she did, no she didn't, yes she did.

At twenty-two, determined to become a painter, a degree in English literature her only training apart from Saturday art lessons at the Boston Museum of Fine Arts, she left her parents' home for the ocean town of Gloucester. There, she'd been told, an artists' colony thrived. By autumn she was sleeping with a man, a painter fifteen years older than her. He'd trained as an architect in Belgrade, then emigrated to Paris to paint and eventually moved to New York, searching for inspiration and hoping to do better.

Gloucester, Yovan warned her, would empty of artists in winter. So she found herself a big room above a wine shop on a New York avenue, and her father paid the rent.

When, in my early twenties, I'd ask about her sex life with Yovan, she'd offer vague answers. Then, one day, she confessed to having decided, in the moment he first 'seduced' her, that theirs had to be a great love to justify her relinquishing her virginity. If theirs was true love, she was not a slut or loose woman. To the idea of their great love she'd remain loyal for over a decade. The ideas we cling to in order to elude shame hold great power over us.

Over the course of ten years, Yovan would change the way she ate and cooked. He'd turn her head toward Europe. When they attended an opening at a gallery they'd arrive separately and leave separately, yet by Yovan she felt shielded, she said, from the visceral American art scene surrounding her.

She led, she said, a 'double life' during her New York years – double because she had a lover but pretended to be single. I say it was a doubly double life, made so by an inner rift. Not only was she pretending to be single, but she was suffering from divided loyalty between two selves. She distrusted her beauty, which had arrived without warning, when she was seventeen, transforming how others treated her. When she allowed herself to enjoy her striking new looks – her sudden ability to inspire avidity in men and jealousy in women – she betrayed the plump and awkward, socially persecuted person she'd grown accustomed to being. Wanting neither to abandon her solitary and truer self, nor to forgo the pleasures and power bestowed by her outward beauty, she existed in a torn condition.

I asked what finally freed her to leave Yovan. She told me she'd been struck, one sunny afternoon – slapped awake by the happiness of a young couple who passed her on the sidewalk. Walking hand in hand, they were laughing. She saw no effort of translation being made and concluded that neither had experienced more of life than the other. No yawning gap of fifteen years separated them. Her time with Yovan was over. She left New York, lived in a New Hampshire farmhouse, painting, then made her way to Paris, on a Fulbright fellowship.

≈

When I was eleven, so the story I usually tell myself goes, and my sister was thirteen and the object of my mother's worry, therefore the object of her attention, I retaliated by mocking our mother. I'd never resemble her, I insisted.

She was interested in clothing. Clothes therefore bored me. Femininity mattered to her. I rejected femininity. Art and literature were her passions. I'd focus on the factual: climb trees and study history.

About who I was, or was becoming, our mother felt less anxious than she did about who my sister was, or was becoming. This left me freer to deviate from our mother's desires. With me she competed less. Christina's criticisms sent waves of panic through our mother. My every breath and word mattered but weighed less than my sister's, and this spared me.

Our mother devoted to us, and to our father, a quiet, steady energy that appeared limitless. She listened to our woes, supplied us with books, art supplies, and encouragement, while also attending to our daily, practical needs. Without complaint she toiled as our cook, maid, and chauffeur. When we were at school and our father was teaching at the university, she'd escape for several hours (daily or not so often?) to her studio to paint and re-become her truest self.

≈

The psychological architecture of our family contributed to Christina's illness, which in turn altered our family's functioning. I should perhaps say illnesses. They were plural. The diagnosis of schizophrenia did not come until she was in her forties. A diagnosis of post-traumatic stress disorder preceded it, in her twenties.

At thirteen she'd become anorexic, but that illness went unnamed until much later.

She also suspected she was on the autism spectrum.

The Christina I remember from childhood was kind to me. In adolescence she grew more distant but remained my generous, studious older sister, who did not complain about my volubility and could often be convinced to engage with me in childlike forms of play.

~

When we were both very young, on those rare days when guests came over, my parents would instruct me to give my sister a chance to speak up.

Our mother, seeing herself in Christina, sought to protect her from me. Our father believed that too loud a public display of any child's ego should be discouraged, so that calm could prevail and adults could enjoy their conversation, and, as he admitted with a rueful smile, so that he in particular might be heard.

I would quiet down and rage inwardly while waiting for my sister to speak, and she would remain silent.

But once Christina reached adolescence she could no longer remain silent. Our father's views offended her too deeply. The illogicality he at times displayed, when in the grip of emotion, she judged unpardonable in a mathematician. He claimed to be a person of logic yet denied his inconsistencies. What's more, he obstinately refused to admit the soundness of her claims. She could neither win the argument nor escape his mental bullying – so she felt.

She and our father fought fiercely, and I, unnerved by their battles, decided to remain a child for as long as possible, and to place safety before logic.

~

'*Familiar*,' she'd note in her journal, 'is a word I allow. *Family* is not.'

On the day she moved into her basement apartment, a set of rooms entirely her own, her spirits were high. She brought few belongings, mostly books and art supplies, leaving the bulk of her possessions in storage at our mother's house. Together she and I had gone to IKEA to choose her a table and chair.

Her apartment opened onto a tiny front garden, and though the garden left Christina indifferent – as she could not imagine sitting outside on display, not even with a book to hide behind – nevertheless the existence of the garden reassured me, as if I were the one moving in.

As I got in my car to drive away, Christina expressed again her gratitude for my help.

Over the next several months I refused to provide our mother with an answer when she'd ask, as she did each time I visited: 'Why won't Christina speak to me?'

In response to my evasive silences, our mother would express perplexity: 'I keep going over everything I said to her. But I can't figure out what wrong word I used or what I did to offend her. Unless it was "boutique hotel"? Is that why she won't speak to me?'

Eventually my resolve to protect our mother crumbled. I explained, as best I could: 'She's unwell and believes that you tortured her when she was a child. It is her illness speaking. At the moment she's too unwell to see you. She needs space. She's asking to be left alone.'

Our mother insisted on writing Christina a note. 'I have to tell her I love her. I want her to know that I would never have intentionally hurt her.'

I tried to convince her that her message would only intensify Christina's distrust: 'You'd do better to express your love by exercising self-restraint and not intruding.'

Such advice was easy for me to give, hard for her to receive. Our mother's face filled with anguish each time I refused to deliver her note. My sorrow for our mother grew. I too was a mother. That Christina felt she had the right to accuse our mother of torture, then retreat, flinging instructions over her shoulder, barring our mother from telling her side of the story, angered me. I therefore relented and agreed to act as messenger.

When my sister and I next met for coffee, I slid a small envelope across the round table between us. We were seated on a College Street patio, and from behind the flat rooftops across the street, mountainous white clouds rose, swelling in the blue sky. I said: 'You won't want this. It's from Mom, telling you she loves you. I felt sorry for her and agreed to give it to you. I don't care if you read it or tear it up. That's up to you.' Christina shoved the envelope into her capacious book bag.

The following day she left me a voice message. I must not attempt to contact her again, she said, not for the foreseeable future.

I reported to our mother that I would be making no further efforts at communication with my sister and that I recommended she too respect Christina's desire to be left in peace. Our mother agreed not to interfere further. She had no choice. She knew neither my sister's address nor her cellphone number.

Several months passed and I began writing a novel. To do so I turned myself into a teenaged German boy named Heinrich. I went back in time to the 1970s, and chose as my home Tettnang, a village near the Bodensee, surrounded by hops fields and orchards. To Heinrich I gave an older sister, Inge. Though fond of her younger brother, Inge considered him a bit of a pest. He was a slow reader but an avid walker. She gave him the diaries of the eighteenth-century British explorer Samuel Hearne. Inge recommended that Heinrich take a hike. A long one. He should go to the Canadian Arctic. His doing so would keep him out of her hair.

Within a year of completing high school, Heinrich would follow Inge's advice, fly to Iqaluit, then to Pangnirtung, and from there set out on foot. For practical reasons, I'd decided that my protagonist would not go to the Western Arctic, where Hearne had been, but would hike instead on Baffin Island. I planned to accompany Heinrich, so his route had to be one I could imagine undertaking, and I knew of Auyuittuq National Park. My trek would last two weeks. Heinrich, however, would not emerge from Auyuittuq (in Inuktitut, *the land that never melts*) until thirty years after setting out. He'd find himself flung radically into the future, without having aged. His trek, from 1980 to 2010, would fill his ears forever with the rushing sound of glaciers melting, a roaring warning from which he could no longer be free.

Heinrich's story would end with him making his way from Pangnirtung to Toronto to search for his sister. She'd now be thirty years older than him. In a letter Inge had written and left for him at the Parks Canada office, when she'd come from Germany to Pangnirtung, unwilling to accept that his disappearance meant he'd died, she'd said she was headed for Toronto next, and that he should come join her if he was alive, which he had to be, since he was reading her letter.

As Heinrich wandered the streets of Toronto, daily his hope of locating his sister diminished. But one afternoon, there she was – exiting the Toronto Reference Library. He pursued her down Yonge Street.

Within a few weeks of my reuniting Heinrich and Inge within the pages of my manuscript, I received a phone call from our mother. Full of disbelief and excitement, she announced that she'd spoken with Christina, who had decided to end her long period of isolation. Had they spoken in person or by phone? I don't recall and can ask neither of them now.

Right when Heinrich and Inge found each other, Christina, needing to escape her apartment, had decided to find us. Infestations of centipedes occur any time – meaningless coincidence was at work, not some mysterious force organizing our lives, stated my rational mind. Yet I could not resist imagining that my sister reappearing in 'real' life the moment Heinrich spotted Inge in my novel might be a sign. But a sign of what?

When writing a novel, often I hope for an indication, however oblique, that I am on a path leading to a truth, however elusive.

Once, I created a psychiatrist and gave him a dream. In his dream a splendid tree – its leaves dark green and its abundant flowers pure white – stood by a fast-flowing river. All at once the flowers flew off. In reality they were birds. The psychiatrist woke, drenched in sweat, convinced that all the women he loved were poised to leave him.

The psychiatrist lived, I'd decided, in Paris. To check on certain facts about the city, I travelled there and had dinner with a man who was a real psychiatrist, a family friend I'd known since I was eighteen. Partway through the meal, his wife, who was dressed entirely in white, left the room. When she returned, a white pigeon was perched on her arm. The bird, she explained, had fallen from its nest when it was still too young to fly, and had been rescued by her husband. The bird had become so attached to the psychiatrist that it would follow him when he did his rounds at the hospital, swooping down hallways, waiting outside rooms it could not enter. That a bird was permitted in the corridors of a Paris hospital strikes me as less than credible, yet I'm certain that's what she told me.

'The truth about stories is that that's all we are,' says Thomas King.

≈

During her several-year stay in her second-to-last home – the semi-detached house perched on a rise, to which she'd fled from her basement apartment – Christina, by then in her fifties, produced a continuous flow of poetry and visual art.

Her most frequent walking destination was the Toronto Reference Library. Countless books on conceptual art and collections of poetry called to her from the shelves. Slowly, eagerly – slowing her pace to contain her eagerness, and on other days slowed by despondency or physical exhaustion – she moved between the rows, reading the spines. Hers had become a heavily medicated existence. Twice a week, she was seeing Dr. R.

The books that intrigued her she'd pile on a table for closer examination. Hours passed while she copied sentences into notebooks.

A list on a loose page fell from one of her notebooks a few months ago, when I lifted the notebook from my desk. At the top of the list she explains that a work of hers, titled *Mutilated Are*, includes:

reversed text by (or in the case of art criticism concerning) the following:

Michael Palmer, Peg Boyers, Georgia O'Keeffe, Margery Sharp, Mark LeVine, El Anatsui, Alice Notley, Niels Frank, Marjorie Welish, Suzanne Robertson, Rachel Rose, Mari-Lou Rowley, Lisa Robertson, Michael Dickman, Joyelle McSweeney, Lyn Hejinian, Antonin Artaud, Fernando Prats, Liliana Porter, Adam Pottle, Sasha West, Juliana

Spahr, Karen Volkman, Steve McCaffery, Sina Queyras, Clea Roberts, Heather Pyrcz, Marquard Smith, Ann Lauterbach, Mary Jo Bang, Ken Babstock, Alice Fulton, James Galvin, Forrest Gander, C. S. Giscombe, Elizabeth Robinson, Stephen Ratcliffe, John Yau, Dean Young, Eleni Sikelianos, Rod Smith, Rosmarie Waldrop, Leigh Kotsilidis, Gillian Savigny, Carmen Giménez Smith, Keith Waldrop, Kent Monkman, Jenny Holzer, Joshua Mehigan, Erin Belieu, Jorie Graham, Gertrude Stein, Claire Lacey, Kaie Kellough, Kevin McPherson Eckhoff, Richard Krueger, Erín Moure, Jay MillAr, Gary Kibbins, Ana Rewakowicz, Germana Matta Ferrari, The Minus Times Collected (various contributors), John Ashbery

Mutilated Are I've not yet located. I'm unlikely ever to locate and read *Mutilated Are*. The days when I dare open Christina's journals and manuscripts are few.

≈

Our encounters over coffee, always in the same café, to discuss art and books, began during those years that she lived in her semi-detached house, with its much inscribed walls, her painted words intended to keep humans out.

Nearly always she'd tell me of an artist I'd not heard of. Straight away I'd find their work online and borrow books from the library. I'd thank her for inviting me to see through the eyes of Christian Boltanski or Rachel Whiteread, to feel with their nerves, to glimpse their thinking. Every artist whose work she introduced me to I'd return to repeatedly, seeking sustenance. And I too put forward names. Had she heard of Brian Jungen or Nadia Myre? They both blew my mind. What would she make of William Kentridge?

He'd designed sets for Gogol's *The Nose*, which had apparently been made into an opera.

The works of artists were bread crumbs we dropped on the forest floor so we could find our way back. Back to where?

≈

Several times a week Christina would make the ten-minute walk from her house to our mother's. She'd go in the afternoon and read aloud to our mother, who was losing her eyesight. Whatever book our mother selected, Christina saw in our mother's selection a covert message embedded and addressed to her. 'Mom wants to destabilize me. That way I can't tell on her. I can't spill the beans.'

After their reading session, the two would share a light meal. I'd buy the food, and Christina would warm it up and leave a list for me when items got low. 'Don't count on me,' Christina would warn. 'I'll go see Mom when I can. But sometimes I won't, because I can't.'

More days than not she went. Many months passed. Over a year elapsed. Then our mother fell in the night, left her house, and would never return to it.

≈

Not long after our mother's fall, I knocked on Christina's door. It had become my habit to drop by once or twice a week and ask how she was doing. She took me around to the exposed side of the house and showed me an inch-wide gap between the wall of the house and the concrete retaining wall intended to prevent the basement from shifting. We'd been informed at the time we bought the house that the basement wall had moved in the past. We'd chosen to trust that the problem had been resolved.

The following day, I brought a builder. He determined that the basement wall could not be trusted and advised us to replace it as soon as possible. For how many years might the wall last if we did nothing? He could not say. Were a neighbour to notice the gap and alert the city, an inspector would be sent, he warned. The city would require that the basement be repaired. We could, of course, cover the gap so no neighbour saw it. But the house would still be resting on a faulty foundation.

This news angered Christina. She did not trust the builder, accusing him of exaggerating the problem so that we would hire him to undertake an expensive reconstruction. I consulted with a second builder and called in an engineer. Both agreed with the first builder.

The prospect of workmen invading her home alarmed Christina. She informed me that she'd been failed. I'd promised her safety but had instead imposed a crumbling house. Neither ignorance nor ineptitude could explain, she said, why I'd refused to take her warnings seriously when we were choosing between houses. Only disrespect of her intelligence, and my willingness to sacrifice her well-being for the sake of expedience, could make sense of how dismissive I'd been. If I imagined she was going to stay put while strange men invaded, I was sorely mistaken. Through my folly she was now trapped in a faulty home. I'd better find her a new place to live, and do so today, not tomorrow. If one more workman knocked on her door, she'd not be able to bear it. I'd trusted my husband instead of her, when he'd voiced his bullshit opinion that the retaining wall would doubtless keep doing its job. Nobody ever listened to her, despite her excellent reasoning. Perhaps the excellence of her reasoning threatened us all? This shifting basement wall was not hers to fix, she'd not caused this catastrophe. I'd better find her somewhere else to live.

She'd been right about the wall. Yes, I agreed. I should have given her warning more weight. But her warning, as I remembered it, had consisted of a skeptical look followed by a few words of doubt tossed into a swirling conversation about the advantages and disadvantages of three houses on offer, and we'd all agreed that the advantages of this particular house outweighed its potential disadvantages. Had she clearly expressed her belief that we were making a mistake and should keep looking, I'd have agreed to continue searching. Wouldn't I?

Whoever was at fault, a solution was required. I proposed that she move, for a trial period, into our mother's house, it being solidly constructed and empty of people.

≈

On the night she got out of bed to pee and lost her balance, our mother lay on the floor unable to get up. Several minutes passed, then she remembered the small device she wore and pressed its button. Alerted by the company that monitored the device, I got out of bed, pulled on some clothes, and cycled over to her house.

The year before, I'd rolled up the carpets and moved them to an upstairs room, so she'd not trip, not on the ground floor. Handrails were installed in strategic places and a hospital bed moved into the book-lined back room so she could sleep downstairs. The tiny washroom off the kitchen met most of her needs. She rarely had to climb to the second floor. She wanted to live in her house on her own for as long as possible, she said.

The fall fractured her shoulder. To monitor her heart, they kept her several days in the hospital. Her shoulder had not yet mended when they decided to send her home. The slightest movement caused her pain. When I pressed them to do better, insisting she was not yet ready to resume living alone, they relented and provided her with a room in the rehabilitation wing of a residence for seniors.

With a graciousness I felt sure I could never emulate, she accepted her new surroundings, made bemused comments regarding the routines imposed on her, and took an anthropological interest in her fellow residents. There was Monica, who'd escaped the firebombing of Dresden by walking, and walking, sticking to small rural roads, staying out of sight of soldiers and begging farmers for food. From Monica our mother learned, she said, how to obtain an extra serving of ice cream at dinner. There was Patricia, a former dog breeder, who'd yell 'fetch' as she hurled her fork and spoon across the room.

Our mother grew accustomed to having someone come to her aid whenever she pushed the buzzer beside her bed, no matter the hour, night or day. She did not mind waiting for her helper to arrive, she said. She trusted they would appear, and if they did not, she could buzz again. 'I'd not realized how frightened I was, living alone. Now I am safe and can relax. There's lots to observe, always someone coming or going.'

To my surprise, she decided against returning to her house. 'If the time has come that I can no longer live alone, I'd rather leave than share my house with someone else. I've loved having my home to myself. Living there with a stranger wouldn't be the same. Since I now need to live with others, I'll do that in a new setting. I'll miss my house very much, but nothing lasts forever.' Her mind was made up. I admired her courage. I stopped looking for a live-in caregiver and began taking her instead on visits to residences for seniors, adding her name to waiting lists for the 'homes' where friends of hers were already settled and could welcome her. The residence where she'd been sent temporarily, to recover from her fall, would 'do for now,' but she hoped for better. Soon a room opened in the home at the top of her list. 'It's not as if I'm losing my house and everything in it,' she reassured herself. 'I can go there to visit, any time.' But she would not go back to visit. She was too wise to do so.

Whenever she thought of something she'd left in the house but wanted, she'd ask me to bring it. 'There's a lacquer box. It maybe has in it the brooch I was given when I graduated from college. This scarf needs something to hold it in place. If I had that brooch. It had a blue stone. While you're there, if you wouldn't mind bringing the photo album, the one with pictures from when I was a child, if that's not too much? I want to see my brother and sister. I think I had a brother and sister, didn't I? I don't know where that album is, but you'll be able to find it, and the complete poems of Emily Dickinson, if that's not too much. Why do I want to read Emily? I guess I just do. Ha! Christina prefers Gertrude Stein. And there should be a black sweater on a chair in my bedroom, or what used to be my bedroom, but the sweater can wait.'

≈

When Christina moved into our mother's house, I laid down a single rule: she was not to write on our mother's walls. Our mother might choose to visit. If she did so, she ought not to find words painted on her walls. They still belonged to her, I argued.

In my sister's own house, the one with the shifting foundation, she'd been free to do as she pleased. The ground floor she'd made into her gallery, the entire space carefully curated, each of her works in conversation with another. Her painted inscriptions began downstairs, climbed the wall beside the stairs, and spread through the second-storey rooms.

Not all her messages were fierce. Behind the clothes in her closet, tiny white letters whispered: 'If Christina.'

Beside the stairs, a life-sized girl, faceless, wearing a checkered dress, gripped the string of a balloon in her rudimentary fist, and on the heart-shaped balloon ten letters spelled out a single desire: 'I want to die.'

Our mother's walls were off-limit. My one restriction. Christina abided by it. She contained her longing to spread language over every surface. Out of fear I might turn her out, or from respect for the logic behind my prohibition, either way, she did not succumb to temptation. She left our mother's walls alone.

Once she'd decided to die, however, she was free to do as she pleased. In preparation for her departure, in a gesture of defiance and liberty, she chose the wall beside her bed as the surface on which to write her final poem:

Because of schizophrenia
Because of The Juniper Tree
Because of losing the house

YOU CAN SAY GOODBYE

3

A narrow room at the side of the house. It had begun as our father's study, then become my bedroom the year I turned nine.

That year, against my will, I'd been removed from Christina's company. I'd been ejected from the large sunny room we shared at the front of the house – a room that was the embodiment of always. Our mother had decided that Christina, balancing on the cusp of adolescence, should be given privacy. 'She needs a room of her own,' said our mother, recalling her own teenaged desire for refuge. In her awkward years of shyness and hormonal rioting, she'd yearned, as eldest child, for a place of escape from her two younger siblings.

Our father moved his study, in a compressed form, onto the porch off our parents' bedroom. The installation of a baseboard heater and glass windows made the porch usable in every weather.

As for my new room (our father's former study), it had an alcove at its southerly end into which my bed fit tightly, and this pleased me. Protected on three sides by walls, I could be attacked from only one direction by the monster that hid beneath. A running leap propelled me through the air, preventing the creature from grabbing my ankle and pulling me down.

When I still could not fall asleep, time crawling and darkness threatening to devour me, our mother would come and perch on the edge of my bed. With the tip of her finger she'd trace the convolutions of my ear's intricate maze, freeing me, slipping me into oblivion. 'There's a little insect in your ear, I'm chasing it, I've nearly caught it, there, I got it.'

My father's immense pine desk, impossible to squeeze into his cramped new study, gobbled much of the room now mine. We could sell it or donate it to a museum, he suggested. It had been designed for use by a row of clerks in an early Ontario post office. I imagined them perched on elevated stools, shoulders hunched – a row of giant birds, their quill pens scratching words into large ledgers. I asked to keep the steeply slanted, impractical desk, so as to keep a part of history, and a part of my father, near me. Not that he'd ever worked in a post office. But he'd laboured on that sloped surface, hour upon hour, with his pencils and rulers.

Also left in my room were low shelves made from boards sanded and stained by my parents. They extended along one wall, each board supported at regular intervals by a stack of several bricks. The shelves held an abundance of dark green books, all identical except for slight variations in thickness. I pulled one out by its spine. It fell open. Nothing but columns of numbers. I flipped the pages, encountered more rows of numbers. Disappointed, I shut the volume and shoved it back in its place.

'What,' I asked my father, 'is inside those books in my room?'

'Mortality tables,' he told me. 'For my work I need to know how many people have died, at what age, in what years.'

In addition to teaching mathematics at the university, he worked as an actuary, preparing pension plans.

'When you're adding up numbers, always use a pencil,' he advised me. 'You'll make mistakes. Everyone does. Use a pencil. That way you can erase your mistakes.'

He was a man who wanted to believe that mistakes could be corrected, who preferred tools that forgave. He had an abiding affection for pencils.

After I left home, my bedroom became the guest room.

The large sunny bedroom at the front of the house our mother would make into a studio when our father died and she was free to paint at home without fear of interruption.

From her parents our mother had inherited a matching pair of single beds with handsome wooden frames. One she'd put in the guest room. The other she slept in after our father's death, until climbing in and out of it became too difficult, she having aged and the frame being high off the floor; then she gave it to me, and together she and I selected a hospital bed for her.

The acorn-shaped finials of the handsome twin beds in which our mother's parents had slept Christina would describe in her journal. When she moved back into the house, the only bed left, apart from a hospital bed on the ground floor, was the one with finials in the guest room, formerly my bedroom, formerly our father's study, and into this small, narrow room she'd fit as many of her dolls, paintings, sculptures, and books as possible.

On the wall of this room she'd write her final poem in blue ink.

≈

What was mine. What was Christina's. My mother, her mother, our mother. My father, her father, our father. My rooms, her rooms, our rooms.

Our disagreement over the house – her desire to claim it, and my resistance to her claim – was in part a battle over whose narration was to win the day, whose telling of the past was to dominate the future. A house is a vessel of memory, of story. In arguing over the house, we were arguing over 'The Juniper Tree' as apt or false telling of our inextricable pasts.

Because of the Juniper Tree

Picture two naked sisters sharing a bath. They are three and five years old, or four and six. The tub is deep and stands on clawed feet made of iron. The small, warm room has filled with steam. The sisters have been soaking, playing with rubber ducks, and have tired of rubber ducks. On a shelf beside the tub lies a hose with a showerhead at one end. It is used by their mother when she washes the girls' hair. The sisters take it from its shelf. Together they yank off the showerhead, then each sinks her end of the hose into the soapy water, into which they've been shedding their dirt and old skin as they soak. Once the hose has filled, each raises an end to her mouth and blows with all her might. Whoever blows the hardest sends grubby water surging into the mouth of the other, who splutters and spits. They begin again, and again. The soundtrack to this tale is wild laughter. One wins, then the other. Loser and winner both delight in the game and go at it again and again.

≈

No photos exist of us with that hose in our mouths, but there are several of us soaking in bathwater up to our waists. Or was it up to our nipples? In these black-and-white shots, taken by our father, I am the one looking down at the rubber duck while Christina's gaze meets the camera lens. Other times the reverse. What I'm describing are not photos but memories of photos. How deep the water was in that tub, I can't say.

A handful of years before taking her life, Christina presented these bath photos to her psychiatrist as proof that our parents had belonged to a ring of pedophiles.

≈

The bathroom of our childhood had one window. It was high up. In summer, I'd balance on my toes, grip the wooden cover of the radiator, hoist myself, unlatch the window, inhale the fragrance wafting from the white-blossomed lilac tree growing from a hole in the stone terrace behind the house. I'd travel out into the flowering night.

To me, from that small room, with its tub, sink, and toilet, a single instance of fear returns. I am very young and call for my mother in the night, wanting her to come and wipe my bum. She rushes down the short hall, steps into the bathroom, and faints at my feet. Yanked suddenly from sleep, she'd gotten out of bed too quickly, causing the blood to drain from her head, she explains to me, sitting herself up on the bathroom floor. The caress of her voice calms me. Perched on the toilet, feet dangling, I ask: and what if I get out of bed too fast, will my head empty of blood? No, she assures me, it won't. And my father? No, he won't faint either. It is only some people who are prone to fainting, she states with certainty. Though I now know something unsettling about her that I did not know before, she looks unchanged. All is well. She gets up from the floor, and I am safe.

≈

Christina, in her early twenties, found a precarious safety in her love of N, and his love of her. Released from a six-month stay in a psych ward (was it six months?), she landed work, thanks to a cousin, as a filing clerk in the back office of a bookstore. There Christina met N, a young man her age, who dreamed of becoming a painter. Her dream was to write. Soon the two were inseparable. Each lived with their parents, each in their childhood home. Both were intent on saving money. They planned to accumulate enough savings to step out of the workforce for a few years, and through discipline and uninterrupted labour launch their careers as painter and writer.

In the hospital, Christina had fallen in love with a young woman, P. Though they were not lovers, their friendship was alive with erotic energy – so Christina felt. Of P's sexuality I know little. From the few times I met her I remember a penetrating gaze, quickness, and a sharp humour. Released from the psych ward, P studied furniture design.

'I have to choose between P and N,' Christina said. We were walking along Davenport to a bus stop at Bathurst (if I'd dropped by our parents' house to collect her), or we were walking along St. Clair to a bus stop farther north on Bathurst (if we'd together left my apartment on Raglan Avenue, which she'd helped me find the year before).

Always Christina and I were walking, and while we walked we were talking. 'Who will you choose?' I asked. 'P or N?'

A few years later, she and N married and moved to the small city of Victoria, on Vancouver Island. There, they could rent for less, stretch their savings, and distance themselves from family. Within a year of their arrival, however, N's parents followed, attracted by the promise of mild winters and delighted not to be separated from their youngest son and his wife.

The four of them moved into a large clapboard duplex built in the era of the queen after whom the city was named. Christina and N occupied the top floor, his parents the ground floor. Immense oak trees shaded the large garden. Once more my sister was living on a corner lot, looking out her windows into the branches of oak trees. She found work behind the circulation desk in a branch of the Greater Victoria Public Library. Being surrounded by books pleased her. Having to interact with her co-workers and the public displeased her. Nine to five, five days a week, N painted. Before dinner they'd walk together along the ocean. All their meals N prepared, and Christina did the washing up.

'I've stopped doing any of the cooking. N was critical of my cooking. So, I've decided that if he doesn't like my cooking, he's better off doing it all. The kitchen is his from now on. That's what he gets for preferring his own cooking. I'll stick to cleaning the dishes,' she wrote to me, or similar words.

≈

We sent each other our news by letter, enclosing our latest stories and poems. We were both hoping to be published one day.

Oct. 23, 1993

Dear Martha,

Telegram. Sorry, I don't have time for more now. I've got to leave to work in an hour (Yuck! Bleck! Oh, well …) I hope my comments re *Fidelity* were O.K., not hurtful. I really love that story! I hope the writing is going well, not too overwhelming, not too frustrating. It's such a comfort and an inspiration to think we are both working away at opposite ends of the country. I'm enclosing some of my poems, plus two short stories I've written over the past week or two (one story, as you'll see, is very short!). I hope you like them. Any 'faves?' 'Non-faves?' ?? I've been writing a lot, typing even more it seems, as I have to keep retyping page after page to get one perfect copy of a story. Sometimes my brain feels as though it'll explode if I don't stop and have a shower or go out for a walk. It's been rewarding so far though. The typing sessions are hard on poor N, because I get very angry and frustrated at all the mistakes I make, and because my writing turning into print puts all kinds of pressure on it, I feel – scary process!! I love my dolls, they make me very very happy. I sent *Uncomfortable Emotions* off to the *Antigonish Review*. Wish me luck.

≈

She'd begun collecting antique dolls. N gardened. She sewed doll's clothes. She read. He read. They searched for treasure at Goodwill and in used bookstores. Preferring each other's company to that of anyone else, they socialized mostly when caught off-guard, or when duty demanded. Their days followed a predictable routine, and this suited them both. 'We live like old people,' they said, and laughed. N had several solo shows in a Vancouver gallery, but his hyperrealist works needed a different audience. He had his eye on New York. The Toronto branch of his Vancouver gallery gave him a show, and though his work received good reviews, sales remained poor. He flew to Toronto to see his sister, her children, his brother, and his gallerist, and a few days later caught an overnight bus from Toronto to New York and walked into the renowned Soho gallery OK Harris, portfolio in hand. The evening of that same day, to spare himself the expense of a hotel, he boarded a bus that deposited him back in Toronto in the morning.

He'd been told by Ivan Karp, the founder of OK Harris, 'Your work is promising. Drop by with your latest next time you're in town.' Two years later, he again caught an overnight bus from Toronto to New York. OK Harris agreed to give him a hallway show. Everything sold. His next show was larger. Everything sold. In his sun porch back in Victoria, hunched over his draftsman's table, he painted daily from nine to five. Derelict neon signs and the graffitied facades of buildings materialized in photographic detail, in watercolour on paper, their realism as unsettling as their melancholy mood. He could not produce his meticulous art fast enough to answer demand. The phone would ring and Ivan Karp's voice would ask, 'So? How many more are ready to ship?'

≈

Meanwhile, letters of rejection from literary journals accumulated in Christina's drawer. Or perhaps she tore them into pieces, burned them, or threw them out, as I was tempted to do with the messages of rejection being sent to me, which instead I filed under the heading 'Responses to My Work.' Part of what kept me writing was Christina's belief in me.

To a friend in Montreal, a poet and journalist, she emailed a manuscript of poems, along with her fears, and asked for his advice. She'd switched, by then, from letter writing to composing emails.

> Thanks ever so for your encouragement re my poetic manuscript! ... I have conflicting feelings about publication – All in all, I'm feeling like a very problematic person these days – I always have

felt this way, of course, but now that I'm no longer trying to self-destruct, I have to find new ways of dealing with my problematic self. I don't seem to be able to exist without issuing challenges of one sort or another – the way I think, the way I write, even the way I dress: none of it fits with what anyone's used to or expects – so I have to either shut up (or try to – I used to be much better at this than I seem to be now!), or find a way of coping with people's consternation.

Seven days later, she emailed him again.

Given the ceaseless raging in my brain, I've decided to sidestep publication – stepping back into the leafy grove of solitary writing, where I'm happy. I hate what happens when society and art meet – not only the way society treats artists, but what I've always seen as artists' complicity in the relationship. I could write a manifesto on the subject, but if I did my inner pacifist would kill my inner anarchist. Thanks once again for your encouragement and solidarity.

Increasingly she turned to her dolls for relief. Their companionship diminished her loneliness. Acquiring and looking after them provided her with a sense of purpose. As passionately as she'd once given herself over to Russian grammar, she now submerged herself in an exhaustive study of the history of European and North American doll-making. Her dolls she adored. By them she felt understood. She named them, gave each a biography, a complex fictional past. She felt quite sure, she wrote to me, that no one comprehended the depth of her connection to them and of their connection to her. What passed between her and her dolls she found difficult to describe to others. 'For better or for worse, my dolls will never be just objects.'

≈

To her husband, N, Christina would speak in the voices of her dolls. Seated on her lap, a selected doll would narrate the events of the day. Some doll's heads were made of wood, others of china.

Miss Moon's was a wooden head. Her black hair, sober blue eyes, and thin red mouth all painted in place, she appeared smooth, poised, self-possessed.

Miss Moon: 'How was my day? I'm so glad you've asked. I've been dying to tell someone. This morning I woke very excited because Christina had promised that today I could try on the new dress she's been sewing for me. She's making it from a pale blue cotton shirt she found at a thrift store. She's designed my dress so that the white flowers embroidered on the cloth climb up across my waist and over my shoulder. The fitting went well. Only a few adjustments need to be made. Christina sat me on a chair right next to her so I could watch. "Sew faster, can't you!" I kept saying in my head, then reprimanded myself for being impatient. Part of my discomfort came from feeling Evie's resentment boring into me, her envy drilling right into the back of my head. Evie's head is made of china. She has a petulant mouth and arched eyebrows of which she's ridiculously proud. What a self-satisfied … You know Evie. You know what she's like. I'm sure Christina's told you how covetous Evie is. Though maybe she hasn't. Christina tries not to say unkind things about any of us behind our backs. But, of course, she can't resist a bit of recreational viciousness. Especially when one of us has been misbehaving and deserves to be mocked. Anyhow, Evie wants my new dress. It wouldn't fit her, since she's half my size, but that doesn't stop her from eyeing it and pummelling me with her unspoken anger. Christina has set aside a scrap of yellow silk to make a purse for Evie, and I'm hoping she'll soon stop staring at me with such disdainful fury and settle into being the proud owner of a silk purse.'

If I concentrate, the words my sister once spoke to me in the voice of Miss Moon return. To place words in Miss Moon's mouth, I've conjured my sister's Miss Moon voice. We are all conjurers.

≈

In what year of her adult life Christina stopped distinguishing between animate and inanimate, I don't know. At some point she lost the reassuring option of perceiving animate and inanimate as discrete conditions of being.

She was nearing sixty when, in a letter to me, she overtly spoke of her mind's 'psychotic screwing with existential categories.' By then she'd been diagnosed with schizophrenia.

We'd together written a book called *Sister Language*, a work of call and response, exploring her relationship to language and mine. It had taken shape quickly, over the course of a year or two. And now it was done. Or almost done. We handed over our manuscript to the publisher, Christina asking that I alone work with the editor. Not a single word of Christina's could be changed, nor any of her punctuation altered. The editor and I were free to delete entire texts and to adjust the order in which texts appeared, but all her words in any included text were to be considered immutable. Her words were literally her. She could be included or excluded but not violated.

While I worked with the editor, honing the shape and flow of *Sister Language*, Christina threw herself into a new project, titled *Packhorse Rosewater*.

One afternoon, she handed me fifteen pages to read:

> rootless, casteless, roofless one wanders ahover over peat bogs, swamps, one's head a bowl carved from mangrove-wood or ... soapstone? Matter not related to the swamps? – hard to tell ... hornbeam? ... no matter, one's head's a bowl, perhaps not carved at all, perhaps potter-hollowed on a hallowed wheel, glazed cobalt or sage – or marjoram-green or a bare or black-pitted brown ... a glaze called peahen? ... one knows one has a fontanel! ... and one arm drags a mangonel – an old (pre-cannon) stone-thrower, a sack of caltrops, a ... what else? A loose assortment of weapon-related objects all somehow held-onto, for whatever reason ... one dreams (half-hearted, bored) of a horse-faced castle a stone's throw from here, of a room-some home ... a largesse of rooms ... theme-bowers? Or themeless? ...

Enthralled by the musicality and playfulness of *Packhorse Rosewater*, I failed to detect in Christina's 'half-hearted' dream of a 'horse-faced castle' a veiled determination to guard her 'largesse of rooms' (our childhood home?) by means of 'a mangonel – an old (pre-cannon) stone-thrower.'

Perhaps such a message did not exist?

'*Packhorse Rosewater*,' she told me, 'is dedicated to you, in thanks for *Sister Language*.'

I felt gratitude and fear, knowing that I could not be who she wanted me to be, not unfailingly. She was finding it increasingly hard to forgive the failings of others, as her own existence became harder, each day presenting obstacles, sorrows, and fears too numerous.

No word in *Packhorse Rosewater* contained the vowels I or U. Except 'pitted,' which had somehow escaped her notice. Blackie – her stuffed bear – had insisted she exclude those two vowels.

She'd brought him down from her bedroom and seated him on a ladder-back chair in the front room of the house, so that he and I could meet. 'Besides Dr. R, you're the only other person to meet Blackie.'

I looked the bear in the eye. The shine of his button orbs returned my gaze. Dressed in a white apron trimmed in blue, he sat very straight.

It was thanks to Blackie that Christina had been able to write *Packhorse Rosewater*, she explained:

> Blackie came up with the idea. He said that since you and I succeeded in collaborating to produce a text Humans want to read, perhaps I could produce a text for Human readers, on my own, without you, if two parts of my brain were to collaborate. There's a part I call Aut, short for autism. Aut's only interested in pattern. But another part of my brain is capable of supplying motivators – bits of language that move a text forward, and forward movement appeals to Humans. They want writing to go somewhere, and aren't satisfied with texts like the ones I produce on my own – texts that are environments, to be entered from any direction. Humans don't get what I do. Blackie's advice has resulted in *Packhorse Rosewater*. Blackie's only requirement is that there be no I or U. He hates those two vowels.

≈

Several months after Christina's death, I began cautiously opening boxes. I was sleeping very little. That I could not alter the past gave the present a metallic taste of pointlessness. The boxes were filled with handwritten journals and ring binders bursting with typed texts, each grouping of texts protected by a plastic sleeve.

On the shiny cover of one thick white binder, she'd inscribed a title: *Dear Martha*. I stared at the paired, incongruous words.

Dear Martha: the weight and thickness of the binder combined with those two words unleashed chaos inside me.

The binder contained an attempted extension of *Sister Language*. She'd interfiled excerpts from her many writing projects with letters addressed to me, elucidating the excerpts. All that was missing were responses from me, which she knew I could not provide unless she showed me the binder. But she'd promised herself to not interrupt my editing of *Sister Language*. Without my participation, the *Dear Martha* binder could not become a work of true call and response, and so she'd tired of it and launched herself, with Blackie's help, into creating *Packhorse Rosewater*.

There's a letter near the start of the *Dear Martha* binder, which I quickly removed and took to a public library to scan, suspecting that I would often want to reread her statements within it, and knowing I'd not often want to face opening the thick binder holding the letter.

In the letter she explains:

I know that one thing my psychotic mind does, is confuse categories to do with the nature of existence: never mind blurring, the lines distinguishing animate & inanimate, human & non-human, hardly exist. Even heavily medicated with an antipsychotic, I still have a hard time believing in those lines. I know how to behave as if those distinctions were clear, but really? – they aren't.

I think that my need to screw with linguistic categories, with syntax & morphology, word order & word formation, is a reworking(-out) in language of my psychotic screwing with existential categories. The psychosis is involuntary & terrifying & inescapable: but the similar language disorder is one I can play with & celebrate: it's creatively fertile. Here I can have some say.

≈

The 'language disorder' to which Christina refers in her letter to me is known as 'formal thought disorder.' This 'disorder' both freed and confined her by causing language to continuously fragment. That neologisms came easily delighted her. However, words breaking apart and recombining without her volition also robbed her of agency and denied her the illusion of safety that a sense of agency can provide. She was at language's disposal – its plaything.

If someone said 'appear,' she'd hear 'app' and 'ear,' causing a Dali ear to enter her vision, or so I imagine. But seconds later 'appear' would split into 'app' and 'pear,' causing a Cézanne pear to replace Dali's ear on the canvas of her mind.

Was it Cézanne's apples or his pears that our mother so admired?

Carrying on a conversation required that Christina suppress the decomposing of language. This took energy. To focus on specific words being spoken to her required that she limit the continuous crumbling and reassembling of words in her ears. Oral exchanges were exhausting. They were exercises in battling her mind's need to free language from fixity.

Hers was a quantum experience of our human universe of words. In James Joyce's *Finnegans Wake* she could relax. There she felt liberated from the false rigidity imposed on language by most humans.

≈

Two decades ago, a letter arrived. I pulled its folded pages from an envelope postmarked Victoria. At that time, besides dolls, Christina was collecting tintype photographs, almost exclusively portraits of women. Because of a photographed glance – a charged look of longing connecting two women – she'd decided to end her marriage, so her letter to me confided. She felt as those two women did. Their visible desire she shared. She therefore had no choice but to leave N, however much this would hurt him. A look of hunger captured by a camera over a hundred years ago left her no choice.

Were both women seated in one photograph, sharing a sofa, Eros in their eyes? Or did desire fly between two photographs taken at different moments, in separate settings, one woman looking from the left page of the album, the other gazing back from the opposite page? I've lost Christina's letter so can't reread her description of the trajectory of that glance full of appetite.

'I can't go on suppressing who I am. Not now' – these words I'm lending her.

Her marriage to N was over. She left him and explored her sexuality. Doing so exhilarated her. But after a few relationships, each of short duration, she declared Victoria's lesbian community claustrophobic. Hoping for greater anonymity, she returned to Toronto.

≈

Her quest for anonymity landed her back in the house of her childhood.

Mother. Language. Body. House. The woman who'd once carried her in her womb now hungered to swallow her headfirst – or so Christina believed, prey to a most ancient fear.

In her twenties, following her first suicide attempt, Christina had accused our father of molesting her when she was a young child. What he'd done to her she could not say, since trauma had erased from her memory what she literally could not live with, she explained. That she'd been violated in unnameable ways – of this she felt certain. Not until later would she include our mother among those who had tortured her when she was small.

Though I'm unable to corroborate Christina's Grimmest narrations, her accusations tie me to an ongoing search for strands of truth woven into the tales that tormented her – tales in whose laboratories she was subjected to ever more sadistic acts, performed by an increasingly elaborate network of enemies, whenever her illness intensified.

Schizophrenia, over time, tailored Christina's past – measuring, cutting, pinning, stitching a skin-tight suit of horror from the fabric of her childhood. In what exact year this tailoring began, I can't say.

≈

If our father molested her when she was a child. If – I hold to uncertainty. When she was alive, my doubting of my sister's accusations contributed to her suffering. And still, I say: if.

On small pads of paper, in her seventies, our mother noted down her dreams.

She was attending lectures by Marion Woodman, a Jungian analyst, whose books fascinated her, as did those of Joseph Campbell, who examined world mythology through a Jungian lens.

On these small pads of notes our mother also recorded small events.

She's come, she says, upon a box of Christmas ornaments made long ago by Christina and me. Seeing them, she asks herself if our youthful happiness was all a performance.

If what Christina now believes occurred, if Donald truly abused her, then how did I not know? she asks.

It was Donald's honesty, our mother reflects, that drew her to him – his open avowal of the impotence he'd experienced with other women before meeting her, a problem she'd clearly cured him of, he pointed out. She'd fallen in love, in part, with his candour and his trust in her.

My mother's notepads tell me nothing definitive regarding what my father, Donald, did or didn't do to my sister. They tell me that our mother had no conscious memory of my father molesting my sister, and in this they contradict my sister's belief that our mother encouraged our father to make Christina the object of his lust, and that she did so to free herself from her husband's sexual attentions, which she did not want, according to Christina.

≈

Dr. R's decades of experience – many of her patients survivors of abuse – did not lead her to believe in what Christina called 'my past.' Naturally this angered Christina, who would fire Dr. R now and again, then return to her. Christina, in Dr. R's opinion, 'did not present' as a victim of sexual abuse.

Had Dr. R treated my sister two decades earlier, might she have encountered a patient who 'presented' differently? The diagnosis my sister was given in her twenties was post-traumatic stress disorder. Much later came the diagnosis of schizophrenia. Did untreated trauma unleash the schizophrenia? This question Christina asked herself. But she came to believe that schizophrenia had been present within her all her life. She held to the accuracy of both diagnoses given to her. Trauma as well as schizophrenia had been ever present.

If our father was the source of her trauma, what exactly had he done to her? To ask myself if my father was my sister's molester requires that I place him at a distance, that I become a clinician in a clinic run by my sister. It is only her beliefs that make me dissect the past in search of sexual crimes.

Possessing no memory of what had been done to her, but convinced that I'd borne witness, she hoped I'd supply her with the memories she'd lost. One of the functions she assigned to me was to corroborate her story.

'All is function' became Christina's motto in her later years.

≈

Walking my bicycle along College Street, about to cross St. George, I heard my phone ring and ignored it. But the sound insisted. I reached into the wire basket on the back of my bike, extracted the phone from my book bag, pressed the small device to my ear, and heard sobbing.

'I have a pain in my chest. I'm scared I may be having a heart attack,' said my mother. 'Christina just stormed out of here, furious with me. She says she's never coming back.'

My mother was in her nineties and still living on her own. I asked her to describe more precisely the physical symptoms she was experiencing. Her heart had been racing and she'd felt short of breath. This combination of sensations she'd experienced at other times with no severe consequences. I said that I'd cycle right over, but if she felt a tightening or pain in her chest she should call 911 immediately. And yes, I'd ride carefully.

Moments earlier, when my phone rang, I'd been walking my bicycle instead of riding it, attempting to calm myself in the wake of a strange event. I'd just emerged shaken from Convocation Hall, an old and round and large theatre on the University of Toronto campus.

A long program of short performances by a wide variety of artists was taking place that day, a Sunday in October. A pianist I admired had been scheduled to play and so I'd bought a ticket, planning to hear her, then skip all the other performances, the weather too gorgeous to stay cooped up indoors for more than an hour at most.

As soon as I entered the hall, a memory of me fleeing the same theatre, over thirty years earlier, had sprung into vivid existence, as if projected on a screen inside my head.

I'd been eighteen years old when I'd fled. That academic year, my second, I'd signed up for an introductory course in psychology. The Psych 101 lectures were attended by hundreds of students and delivered in Convocation Hall. I'd found a seat in the crowded theatre, had raised my eyes to the screen behind the professor, and been confronted by a projected image of a very fat mouse. He or she stared down at me through wistful eyes. The mouse had been placed on a scale and was being weighed. Researchers, the professor explained, had removed a tiny portion of the animal's brain to find out what area allowed it to know when its stomach was full. Once the scientists had snipped out the relevant cells, the mouse could no longer stop itself from eating. Had the scientists not taken away its food, the subject of their experiment would have kept gobbling until his or her stomach exploded. Looking up into the mouse's face, I felt the blood drain from my head. The horror of what had been done to the innocent animal spread through me. I lowered my head between my knees to stop from fainting. Seconds passed. I straightened up. Mouse eyes met my gaze. The helpless rodent sat on the scale, waiting obediently to be lifted in the air and set down elsewhere by a large human hand. Grabbing my book bag, I fled the theatre.

Today a pianist was to perform, and I was no longer eighteen – of these facts I reminded myself as I climbed the stairs to look for a balcony seat. On the long-ago day-of-the-mouse, my seat had been on the main floor, so this time I headed for the balcony. Planning to slip out unobtrusively at the end of the pianist's performance, I chose a seat at the end of a row.

Soon the piano recital began. The pianist's playing thrilled me and ended too quickly. She'd performed half an hour at most. Applause filled the hall. Already the next act was being announced.

'Please welcome acclaimed magician Benito Gianotti.' I'm christening him Benito Gianotti, as I've no recollection of his true name.

A short man, wearing a velvet tuxedo several sizes too small, stepped onstage. Out of curiosity, I decided to linger. I'd not seen a magic show since I was a child.

Either Benito had outgrown his clothing or his clothing had shrunk since he'd last performed. While he thanked the audience for attending, I wondered if he'd intentionally chosen clothing that didn't fit, as a ploy, to distract us from whatever he didn't want us to see his hands doing.

The act we were about to witness was rarely performed, he told us. He asked his assistant – a pretty young woman, of course – to join him onstage. 'And now,' he explained, holding out a pin cushion for us to examine from a distance, 'I am going to stick a pin in my assistant's eye. It won't hurt her, I assure you.' His words entered my ears and filled my head with emptiness.

I have always hated any discussion of eyes. From our mother, I acquired, early on, a fear of losing my sight. This fear she'd learned as a child, obliged to wear thick spectacles with lenses made of real glass. Repeatedly she was warned not to run or catch a ball. Were she to trip or be struck in the face, a shard from her shattered glasses could pierce her eye, she was told.

Sensing I was about to plunge into darkness, I didn't wait to witness the magician insert a pin in his assistant's eye, but got up from my seat, hurried down the winding stairs to the main floor, ran along a curved corridor, pushed on a pair of heavy doors, and stepped into the cool air of a bright autumn day.

For a second time in my life, overwhelmed by thoughts of torture, I'd fled Convocation Hall. I unlocked my bicycle and, not fully trusting my ability to balance, decided to walk down the street rather than ride. Hearing my cellphone ring, I answered and heard my mother weeping.

As I rode up the stone path that led to her house, already she was at the door. I leaned my bicycle against the wall. Together we went indoors. Seated on her sofa, she answered my questions as best she could, pausing now and again to wipe her eyes between sentences and to calm her breathing. This much I learned:

Christina had dropped in, as she did once or more a week. On her way, she'd bought two pastries at a local bakery, one for our mother and one for herself. She'd plugged in the kettle and made a pot of tea. She'd asked how our mother had spent her morning. Our mother had answered that she'd received a phone call from an agitated friend, J, who'd described in great detail an eye operation she was soon to undergo. 'I wish J had spared me the details,' our mother told Christina, 'but I didn't feel I could interrupt, she so clearly needed to talk.'

Christina, perhaps anticipating that our mother might describe, at any moment, the details of J's imminent surgery, leapt from her seat in a fury.

'No matter how many times I tell you not to speak to me about eyes, you go right ahead. I'm done with you. You can't be trusted. I'm leaving.'

She went out the front door. At the bottom of the steps she turned to glare at our mother, who stood stricken in the doorway.

'If you can't behave, I'm never coming back.'

All this our mother related to me in fragments. I stroked her frail arm and held her hand. I could not remember our mother having ever stormed out of a room, as Christina had just done, threatening never to return.

I left our mother, cycled to Christina's house, climbed the steep concrete steps, and knocked on her door. She allowed me into her front hall. Already words were rushing out of her, words propelled by an anger she could not conceal. Having her emotions reveal themselves against her will devastated Christina – so she'd told me more than once. I stood and listened.

'I went to visit her. We were having tea. I'd brought us each a pastry. She started telling me about J's eye operation. All she has to do is mention eyes and I lose it. She knows this. She brings up eyes as a way of disarming me, of maintaining her control. No matter how often I prohibit the subject of eyes, she brings them up, she slips them in. She can't stop herself, can't resist the pleasure of watching me fall apart.'

She paused to catch her breath. I wanted her to continue talking, so I nodded and kept silent.

'There's a reason Mom can't resist going on about eyes whenever we're alone. Its her way of shrinking the distance between me and what she did to me when I was little. If she can shrink that distance enough she knows she'll have me in her power again. I was three years old and Mom was mending a tear in a shirt. Or maybe she was sewing a button back in place, I don't remember which. I was playing with my doll. I must have knocked her arm. She told me to be more careful. I bumped her a second time. To punish me for not holding still, she stabbed me in the eye with her sewing needle.'

Disbelief must have shown on my face. Christina's tone became more vehement.

'It was no accident. She intended to blind me. But she got frightened of being found out, so, to conceal her crime she took me to the hospital, where a surgeon repaired my damaged eye. She told everyone that I'd been operated on because my left eye wandered. A lie, repeated over and over, can be mistaken for the truth. She repeated her story over and over. It's what you and I were told.'

'I'll urge Mom,' I said, 'to not speak to you about eyes.'

'Tell her that if she behaves, I'll talk to her again. But she has to behave. She has to control herself, or I won't have anything to do with her. There were other tortures too. Involving insects. Live insects in orifices. But I'll spare you those. I try to spare you. I try to protect you from my past, I swallow a lot to protect you.'

I left my sister's front porch, descended the steep concrete steps, and walked without purpose, first down one street, then up another and around in a large circle, Christina's desire to be believed pursuing me with animal ferocity.

≈

I am closing my eyes to better see Christina, aged three, taken to the hospital. There, a surgeon will operate on her left eye to prevent it from wandering.

I see a girl who has been separated from her parents. She is made to lie on a narrow gurney. A stranger, oddly dressed in a gown and mask, wheels her into a room where more strangers, gowned and masked, surround her. Immense multi-faceted lights hang close above her. In a picture book about insects she has seen the multi-faceted eye of a housefly magnified. The huge suspended lights remind her of the eye of a giant fly. She is told that the thing being placed over her mouth and nose will not hurt. She must breathe in, then out, and she will tumble into a deep sleep from which she will wake to find that all is well. She obeys. She sleeps, then wakes, as promised. Her parents appear, one on either side of her. Their familiar voices pronounce words that gradually become intelligible. They ask how she is feeling. They tell her she must stay in the hospital overnight, where she will be safe, and that they will return in the morning to take her home. The next day her parents take her home.

All the fear this story contains entered my sister's body and lodged inside her, waiting to feed other fears later.

Within Christina's mind, over time, a chemistry occurred between an actual eye, metaphoric sight, and the first-person pronoun, *I*.

Our mother, as most mothers do, wished to shape her daughters' views. She tried to adjust the lens through which her daughters saw the world. Many parents try to blinker their children. They strive to instill in their offspring a picture of the world with which they themselves are comfortable, eliminating from their children's view elements that cause them – the parents – unease. In this sense our mother desired to blinker her daughters. This blinkering Christina translated into blinding.

The instrument of violence was the metaphoric needle our mother used to stitch her own perceptions, to sew together her most ardently held views, to mend the torn garment she regarded the world to be.

That Christina felt stabbed in the *I* makes sense to me. A story exists in my head. It goes like this:

A girl child, quick-minded, quiet, a dreamer, apt to emerge slowly from her inner world, startled by any sudden demand that she engage with others, is perceived by her mother as needing protection, more protection than ordinary, less sensitive children require. This girl, her parents' first-born, is anything but ordinary in their eyes. Conceived by a woman forty years old, in a time before ultrasound, already as a fetus she becomes an object of concern as well as celebration. Worry hovers. Her safe arrival and good health are perceived as wondrous, a defying of odds. She appears alert, well-formed, eats well, sleeps well. Her parents admire her blue eyes, her high forehead – lots of room in there for brains, proclaims her father. Soon, red-gold hair hangs to her shoulders in thick waves. Her parents resolve to risk a second child. They produce one. This second daughter is dark-eyed, colicky, a non-stop-wailer, and as soon as her little arms grow strong enough she uses them to push at her mother's chest where she will not rest her head the way their peaceful first-born daughter did. This second child's volubility continues beyond infancy. She demands attention. The mother worries that her first-born's quietness may conceal feelings of forlorn displacement. In her eldest daughter the mother sees herself. Vivid memories return to the mother of her own childhood. She recalls being obliged to relinquish her window seat on road trips and to ride in the middle of the back seat instead, wedged between her little brother and littler sister to prevent these two from pinching each other and squabbling. She hears again the voices of adults admiring her younger brother's dimples, her little sister's curls. The eyes of adults pass over her – a tall girl for her seven years, too serious to be adorable, too full of opinion. She wears an immense bow in her hair, thick glasses, and is learning to keep her opinions to herself. She would like to be adored. She would like to be admired for who she is, not expected to incarnate some idea of what a girl should be. She is not allowed to catch a ball or run. She puts on weight. The idea of purity takes hold of her. For several years, hygiene preoccupies her and she washes her hands, her dolls, and many of her other possessions with such ardour and frequency that her mother grows concerned. Gripped by a religious fervour, alien to her parents and siblings, she attends church with strict regularity and takes the necessary steps to be confirmed. Within a few years of her confirmation, the church will cease to offer her what she yearns for. She'll turn away from 'organized religion.' Her quest for a spiritual path will be lifelong, but she does not yet know this. At the end of her adolescence, she'll undergo an unexpected transformation: not only will her eyesight change, freeing her from glasses, but her body will be released from pudgy awkwardness into slender grace. Her beauty and poise will make heads turn. She will both enjoy and distrust her new power over others. It will have arrived so suddenly as to feel unreal. It will detach her from her truer self.

The calm serenity she cultivates will belie her turbulent interior. Her true state, in early adulthood, will be one of anxious questioning and turmoil. From within her fortress of aloof loveliness she will observe the reactions of others and carefully weigh her own responses. She will be fearful of exposing her less desirable self. She knows herself to be inhabited by reprehensible emotions, unworthy of the purity of spirit she aspires to embody. Pride, envy, and anger – when these manifest within her she will attempt to conceal them and to deny their presence.

She has two selves. One holds strong opinions, is fiercely competitive, dissecting, judgmental, ambitious, and this self is strictly silenced, much of the time, by her other self, who seeks to please (her long-dead parents, her husband, her children, her friends) by refraining from argument, by accepting without complaint, and by curbing (or pretending to curb) her desires.

When Christina declared, as she often did, 'our mother is a consummate actress,' I could not disagree. Our mother feared being judged unlovable. And the love she was most scared of losing was the love of her daughters. And the daughter she wanted the most to please was her first, my sister, in whom she saw herself.

≈

My intention was to write about Christina, not our mother. But no sooner did I mention Christina's birth than she disappeared from sight. Contrary to plan, I've just painted a cameo of our mother. Christina vanishing is perhaps the most accurate story I can tell of my sister's childhood. An accurate account of her childhood might go like this: she becomes invisible to herself, she slips from the grasp of her own narration, she is swallowed by the stories that her mother and father tell about her and about themselves; she feels she's a person of someone else's invention.

Bombarded by attention, she feels unseen. Certain forms of attention, she's discovering, erase us.

I remember being shown, one sunny day in childhood, how to burn a hole in a sheet of paper by tilting a magnifying glass at just the right angle to make the sun's rays converge. First a brown dot appeared, small as a pinprick. From this heat prick, a tendril of smoke curled into the air, delivering its acrid smell to my nose. Then the paper burst into flames.

≈

Ineluctable modality of the visible: at least that if no more, thought through my eyes. Signatures of all things I am here to read, seaspawn and seawrack, the nearing tide, that rusty boot. Snotgreen, blue-silver, rust: coloured signs.

In Joyce's *Ulysses*, Stephen Dedalus, walking along the shore, ponders how fully we can perceive reality by means of our eyes. Whether he's siding with the mystics is uncertain. He famously exhorts: 'Shut your eyes and see.' I would like to ask my sister what she made of this passage. But only now am I reading *Ulysses* and she is gone. Could I have raised the subject of sight without mentioning eyes?

In *Bark*, his book on Auschwitz-Birkenau (Auschwitz-The-meadow-where-birches-grow), the French philosopher and art historian Georges Didi-Huberman writes:

The philosophers of the pure idea, the mystics, of the Holy of Holies think of the surface as merely a disguise, a lie: *that which conceals* the true essence of things. Appearance versus essence, or semblance versus substance, in short. One can think, on the contrary, that the substance said to transcend all surfaces is nothing but a metaphysical illusion. One can think that the surface is *that which falls* from things: that which comes from them directly …

The bark is no less true than the trunk … Bark is irregular, discontinuous, uneven. Here it clings to the tree, there it disintegrates and falls into our hands. It's the impurity that comes from things themselves. It tells of the impurity – the contingency, the variety, the exuberance, the relativity – of all things. It lies somewhere in the interface between a transient appearance and a lasting inscription.

≈

The verbal picture our mother painted for me, when I was eight (or ten, or twelve), of the eye operation Christina had undergone as a small child, featured a kitchen stool and a kitchen sink. Stool and sink sprang to the foreground in response to my asking: 'Was I frightened at her being gone overnight? Did I miss her?'

'No,' said our mother. 'You were delighted. While I cleaned the dinner dishes, ordinarily Christina played at being my helper. I'd fill a tub with sudsy water, place it beside the sink, and bring the kitchen stool for her to stand on. She'd clean a doll-sized set of cups and saucers. The night she spent at the hospital, you laid claim to the kitchen stool and took her place. You were happy to have her out of your way.'

Already at the age of one I wanted to get rid of my sister. And, at times, she wanted to do away with me.

One evening, our mother was preparing dinner, perhaps frying an onion in a skillet, when she heard a sharp declaration made by a small voice behind her. 'Fuck off,' Christina had just told me, and the sensation of saying 'Fuck off' had given her such pleasure that she repeated her advice to me, while our mother listened in shock.

Our mother had never said the word *fuck*. Not aloud. She had never formed the word *fuck* with her mouth and released it. Our father called the school to inform them of the vocabulary his daughter was acquiring in their care.

For every time Christina wanted me to fuck off, and for every time I ran at her, head down like a bull, and she raised her knee and knocked me out, there were six or ten or twenty times that we agreed to be sea captains, made a boat from overturned chairs, and together sailed away.

4

At twelve she heard her first auditory hallucination. Our father's voice spoke to her from inside a large oak tree. She wanted to die but couldn't end her life because she believed she was the air our mother breathed – so states a journal entry, written in her fifties.

At twelve she told no one that she'd heard a tree speak. At twelve she told of her suffering by refusing to eat. Two years later her appetite returned.

At sixteen she began cutting through her skin with a razor, inscribing her pain on her forearms. This ritualistic practice made her feel alive, she said. It brought a measure of relief, it calmed her. I, not she, am attaching the word *ritual* to her repeated acts of slicing and her avowed pleasure in tasting her own blood.

There was a lust in her that frightened me when I was fourteen and she sixteen. At fourteen, all lust, including my own, scared me. She told me of the use she'd found for our father's razors. Her confession frightened me. It opened a door into unfathomable darkness.

If it was summer, she was wearing short sleeves. We were in the book-lined back room, its windows overlooking the stone patio and the long narrow yard shaded by huge oak trees. If it was winter, then she must have inadvertently or deliberately pushed up her sleeve. Our mother saw the scars on her arm and asked how they'd come to be. 'I fell,' Christina answered. Our mother left the room. I'd been half listening. Now I turned my full attention on my sister, walked over to her, and there they were: several thin red marks. They did not look like the result of a fall.

'What really happened?' I asked.

'I cut myself with Dad's razors.'

'Why?'

'Because I like the taste of my blood.'

She must have seen fear in my eyes.

'Don't tell,' she warned. 'If you tell, the whole family will fall apart.'

I debated what to do. I consulted with Christina's closest friend, G, a girl I also knew and greatly liked. We decided to tell. But not my parents. That way the family wouldn't fall apart. We decided to tell G's mother, who assured us she'd speak with my sister. Some time later G's mother reported to us that she'd given Christina a choice: she must see a therapist or our mother would be informed that she was cutting herself. Christina had then failed to show up at the therapy appointment arranged for her by G's mother. This meant, I concluded, that our mother now knew, and all could now be worked out between my mother and my sister. I'd done all I could, I told myself, and I turned my attention away from my sister's incomprehensible violence, as if it were a monster eager to devour me. Her desire to hurt herself made her opaque, threatening. She'd attached our father to her actions by using his razors, and she'd lied to our mother. This veiled, blade-wielding new sister I did not want to know. I swore never to resemble her. I raised a wall to keep her out. I waited for my true sister to return.

The following year, I learned from Christina that she was now cutting her thighs. They offered more room, more scope. The gashes both widened and grew in length. She lived in fear, she said, that her blood might soak through the bandages and stain her clothing.

'Where do you do it?' I asked. 'In your room? In the washroom?'

'No. G's room. I have a key. She gave it to me.'

G, alongside Christina, had entered university that year. Unlike Christina, she was living on campus, in a student residence.

'Does she watch you do it?'

'No. I do it when she's out.'

'Do you still use Dad's razors?'

'I have my own. Or when I don't, I use a broken beer bottle.'

Her tone was defiant, her willingness to answer my questions not an invitation to express concern, or pass judgment, or interfere. My function was to acknowledge.

I did not ask our mother if she knew that Christina was still hurting herself. The sister who sliced her arms and thighs was an alien not to be confused with my true sister, who joked with our mother and me in the kitchen. Together my true sister and I set the table, and after dinner cleared the table, washed the dishes, then climbed the stairs to our bedrooms to do our homework, or settled on the bench in the back room to watch TV.

One day the sister whose routines resembled mine, the playfully inventive sister, familiar to me and easy to claim as mine, rescued a piece of ginger root from our mother's cutting board. It resembled a wild boar. She held it up to reveal its true shape. Little Boar, she named it and made a tiny pillow for it, and a tiny bed of paper towel in which she laid it down to sleep, on a china plate, in the cupboard. Each time she opened the cupboard, she'd ask: 'How have you been? Anything new and exciting to report from inside the cupboard? How does life look from in there?'

With each passing week, Little Boar shrank and shrivelled. The day arrived when, with a calm that shocked me, Christina informed Little Boar that his life was over. 'I'm sorry,' she told him, 'but I have to throw you out.'

And that was the end of Little Boar and his paper-towel bed and paper-towel pillow. I'd open the cupboard and wish he were still there.

≈

When I'd wake at night, needing to pee, and cross the hall to enter the bathroom, always a bar of light would be glowing under her door. She was at her desk – of this I was certain – reading Dostoyevsky in the original, or Goncharov or Bulgakov or Gogol or Akhmatova – most passionately Akhmatova.

At sixteen she was, I now believe, in love with her high school Russian teacher, L, who was probably at most ten years older than Christina. Slender, electric, blue-eyed, and beak-nosed like Akhmatova, L strode through the school's corridors, igniting the air with her urgency.

≈

In a journal entry from the last years of her life, Christina regrets: 'If only I hadn't fallen in love with death when I was so young.'

The sister I picture falling 'in love with death' is seventeen and holed up in her room, translating *Requiem* – Akhmatova's long and extraordinary poem in which she bears witness to the great purge under Stalin.

Christina has completed high school and entered university. Her passions are Russian literature, French literature, Russian grammar, and Old Church Slavonic. No Russian author more recent than Bulgakov interests her; the present-day Soviet holds no allure. Yet her Russian professor, whom she adores, passes her off as a young cousin from Moscow at a party. Christina's remarkable fluency, her mastery of the language in its every nuance, is making her an object of attention. She feels more object than subject. A shiny, brilliant object. Her skill exists for all to admire. And behind her skill, who is hiding? She does not know the answer. All her own poems of that period she models, in rhythm, imagery, and tone, on those of her muse, Akhmatova, many of whose poems she sets herself the challenge of translating. Here is her translation of 'The Guest.'

THE GUEST

Everything's as it was, a blizzard
Of tiny snow-flakes beats against
The window-pane. I am not changed –
Except that a man came to see me.

I asked: 'What is it you want?'
He said: 'To be in Hell with you.'
I laughed: 'Watch out, you'll bring
A curse upon us two.'

But, raising a dry hand, he touched
The flowers in my vase
Lightly: 'Tell me, whom do you kiss?'
Tell me, who kisses you.'

And, gazing at me dimly,
His eyes never left my ring.
In his lucid, evil face
Not a single muscle moved.

Oh, I know what makes him happy:
The knowledge, passionate and tense,

That he needs nothing from me,
That I've nothing to refuse.

For the first time, at eighteen, Christina slept with a man. Or perhaps she did not. She asked our parents for permission to spend a weekend alone with a friend at the family cottage. He was a teaching assistant for a Russian course she was taking. Her request distressed our father. Our mother, however, convinced him to let Christina to do as she wanted. It was important they show trust in their daughter, who was no longer a child. They must give her freedom and have faith in her ability to look after herself.

A few days before she was to leave for the cottage, our father walked into Christina's room. It was late afternoon. She sat studying at her desk. In an agitated voice he told her that she was very beautiful, as beautiful as our mother, that he was worried for her safety, that times had changed since his youth and the freedoms now enjoyed by young women meant he could do nothing to protect her beyond warning her of the callousness of young men. As he spoke, his voice caught in his throat. Possibly tears ran down his cheeks.

This visit from our father she recounted to me years later. His out-of-control emotions had frightened her, she said, and she'd stood rigid, waiting for him to leave, which he had done.

≈

Once, when I was ten or eleven, I heard a sound, turned my head, and saw that my father was crying. We were sitting side by side on the bench in the back room, watching a film on television. A fistfight between two men had erupted on the small screen – was this what was upsetting my father? Quickly he left the room, looking for a Kleenex to dry his eyes and wanting to hide his distress from me. I had never seen him cry before.

~

I know of another film that so troubled him he truly fled. I was one year old (or not yet born) and Christina three (or two), when our parents hired a babysitter for the evening and went to see Bergman's latest, *The Virgin Spring*. In the film, based on a thirteenth-century Swedish folk song, a teenaged girl is raped by goat herders in a forest. During the rape scene, our father whispered to our mother that he felt sick to his stomach, and he left the theatre to get some air. She followed him out to where he stood distraught on the sidewalk.

Did our father see in the Swedish girl, in her trusting and innocent beauty, the lovely teenager his ivory-skinned, blue-eyed daughter Christina would one day grow into?

My father was not alone in finding the film hard to stomach. On November 15, 1960, the *New York Times* critic Bosley Crowther commented:

> When the maiden, sent by her father to deliver candles to the church at Easter time, has been stopped in the forest by the goatherds, then raped and murdered by them ... It is a brutish and horrible offense, which Mr. Bergman has represented for all the hideousness and terror it contains.
>
> The maiden, played by Birgitta Pettersson, is a fresh and lovely thing. The goatherds, played by [Axel] Duberg and Tor Isedal, are brutes. Their deception of the child is nauseating, as is frankly

depicted by the reaction of a boy who is with them and watches the violence done. And when they ravish her, the act is imaged – well, almost too candidly. Although the scene has been cut from the way it was shown in Europe, it is still sickening on our screen.

Mr. Crowther, however sickened, remained in his seat in the darkness of the cinema, watching a black-and-white depiction of rape fill the immense screen.

When Christina, hospitalized following her first suicide attempt, accused our father of having molested her when she was a child, I began searching my archive of memories for evidence to support her claim. I could no longer see my father as innocent, but neither could I find him guilty without knowing what he'd done, and Christina could not tell me. I tried to imagine him penetrating her vagina with his fingers or thrusting his hardened cock into her mouth. He became in these imagined scenes of horror a very different man from the father I knew. Had he raped her, and if so, at what age? My sister's suicide attempt was clear evidence of desperate suffering. If what she believed to have occurred had in fact happened, then by not believing her I would be violently adding to the harm already done to her by our father. But I needed to know more if I was to believe in his crime. I could not decide whose narrative to trust. If I believed my father, I risked betraying my sister. If I believed my sister, I risked betraying my father. Do we choose our beliefs? I was being asked to take a leap of faith.

Our mother, too, was torn. She did as I did, and examined her memories. Two coroners, we laid out the past and attempted an autopsy. But the past was not dead and refused to hold still.

It was during one of these searches for evidence that I learned from our mother of my father's visceral response to *The Virgin Spring*. Together we weighed his reaction to Bergman's film as possible evidence of guilt.

Had a repressed desire to rape his daughter yanked him from his seat and compelled him to leave the cinema? Had he already molested her? Or was he guilty of nothing but seeing a grown Christina in the actress on the screen and of finding it unbearable to watch a brutal rape from which he'd be as unable to protect his daughter as was the father in the film?

≈

A few weeks ago, I found among my mother's papers love letters written to her by my father.

The year is 1956. It is summer. My not-yet-mother is thirty-eight years old and has recently returned from two years in Paris. Now she's back in the USA and trying to figure out how to earn a living while continuing to paint. Whenever possible she's spending time at a girlfriend's apartment in New York. She's telling herself she must look for work, perhaps teach art in a girls' school. But she would rather close her door and stretch a canvas than job hunt, so for now she's living with her brother, her sister-in-law, and their six children in a farmhouse belonging to my future grandparents. When not painting she helps look after her young nephews and nieces. My future uncle, determined to make a living from agriculture, is raising cows, hens, and sheep. On weekends my future grandparents drive out to the farm from their home in a Boston suburb.

Every summer my not-yet-father drives from Toronto to New Hampshire to visit his soulmate, Joe, whom he met at graduate school in New York, decades earlier. His soulmate has married, produced children, and settled in a village from where he commutes to a law office in Concord, the state capital. Joe works long hours throughout the summer, and it pleases him and his wife, Margaret, when my not-yet-father comes to stay and entertains their children by taking them on daylong hikes in the mountains. The children, in eager anticipation of his arrival, have sent him teasing, affectionate letters. They have nicknamed him Uncle-buncle.

Joe and Margaret receive an invitation from friends – my future aunt and uncle – to watch the state primaries on TV. They ask if they may bring along their Canadian house-guest. My soon-to-be-father and soon-to-be-mother collide.

When he composes the love letter below, my smitten father-to-be has decided to break his long drive home to Toronto by spending a night at a Vermont hotel, and in his room he's discovered a convenient supply of complimentary paper.

Wednesday 12th September, '56,

Dearest Mary Jane, how I wish you could have come with me at least this far! The fine dining room that I so admired when the Ransmeiers and I ate here – to-night it was drab, and lonely without you. The fine meal was wasted on me in my dazed condition. And the fine, expensive, room, with an empty twin bed – hah!

Had no idea how nervous I was till after dinner, when the thought of sleep suddenly seemed miles away. Perhaps after writing this I shall relax. If not, I'll write something onto the famous essay on Conservation – which has plagued my conscience for about 8 weeks. It would force my mind off you, but who wants his mind forced away from a vision so beauty-full? Now I'm starting to relax, I think. Just organizing these few words has pulled me out of the daze a little.

As I wound away from Warner, I felt like an explorer who has come upon a new flower, the loveliest man has ever seen. His dilemma: if he tries to take the flower back with him, to make it his flower, the very act may kill it; if he leaves it, another explorer will find it and make it his. And he knows there is no other flower like it. A pure dilemma, classically simple, and – perhaps – tragic. I could weep now, or do any mad thing. But instead I'll go to bed 'to sleep, to dream, perchance to dream' (what, if anything, am I quoting?)

The other night, tired and sickish, I could find my own weird ways to relegate you to a corner of me. But to-night I am full of you. The picture of you being so nice to that elderly lady by her car, with the evening light behind you, and across you, that picture's so wonderfully recorded, forever. You can discount your beauty all you wish, Mary Jane, but that scene was beautiful enough to bring tears to my eyes, right now, as I write. Why am I crying? God knows – it's probably self-pity of some sort. Beauty has never done this to me before. Death has, not the death of my dear ones – never have known it, yet – but the sight of the dear ones to whom the dead were dear.

May be just the relaxing of tension. Did you ever see 'The Long Voyage Home' – based on Eugene O'Neill's sea plays? Do you recall the scene where they forced open the strange seaman's private box and seized the letters in it, and read them aloud, and what the letters revealed? I wept for him – or for me, I suppose, projected in to him. But God knows why now – unless you and I, between us, have wound up my emotional clock to where the spring is almost burst. This is a fine recipe for sleep! What I must do is mail this letter and walk about Norwich and become a part of common humanity again – not that unique mortal who is loved by a goddess, and sits alone to weep about it!

...

Good night, Mary Jane, (my) darling. I'll probably sleep fairly well now, dreaming about the Fair Lady in the Castle on Burnt Hill.

Donald xxxxx

Over the next two years, the explorer will send numerous letters to the flower he's discovered – the loveliest flower man has ever seen. Now and again my future parents indulge in a long-distance phone call. Every chance he gets, he flies to Boston, or to New York, to whichever city she's calling home.

≈

My not-yet-father carries a burden: a failed first marriage. His hidden shame is different from that of the protagonist in *The Long Voyage Home*. In the film, private correspondence is stolen from a merchant seaman by one of his shipmates, who wrongly suspects him of passing information to the enemy in wartime. The correspondence reveals that the seaman is indeed concealing a secret, but not one that makes him a traitor. The letters are from his wife. They tell of his being stripped of his commission as an officer due to alcoholism. She implores him to come home, to leave the merchant marine, which he's signed up for under a false name. She urges him to stop fleeing the truth.

My father, unlike the seaman, was not a heavy drinker. But he knew the pain of living with a private source of shame, and of fearing it might be discovered and made public. His first marriage he'd failed to consummate, unable to perform. Because his wife was Catholic and divorce forbidden her, he had had to apply for an annulment, presenting his sexual failure as grounds for him and his wife to be freed of each other.

≈

'What exactly do you want me to believe?' I asked my sister, when we were both in our twenties. 'What exactly did he do to you?'

'I don't remember,' she answered. 'But I think you witnessed what he did. I think you saw.'

I questioned our father. I was driving the family car down a country road, he in the passenger seat, or we were in the front room of the house, he lowering his newspaper and I pulling a chair close, or we were in other places now erased from memory, when I asked him to explain my sister's anguish, to tell me what he believed had gone wrong when she and I were small? What part had he played?

He spoke of his youth, of his sexuality, of his insecurities, of his experiences during World War II, adding details he'd not previously included in his tales of his time as a naval officer. Whenever the warship of whose radar he was in charge would dock in a harbour after an extended stretch at sea, every man but two would hurry on shore to get laid. One of the two men to stay on board was him.

'The other fellow was a Brit, a devout Christian, and married. His faith wouldn't allow him to break his marital vows. But I had no vows to break. What kept me back was fear. I was scared I'd not be able to perform.'

Returned home, the war abruptly over, my not-yet-father shoved his fears aside and married. Within eight months, his marriage was over. At the height of his stress, one evening, before or after the annulment, snakes slid out of the wall in front of his desk. By concentrating on a mathematical theorem, he forced the snakes to retreat back out of existence. He was grateful, he told me, to have hallucinated only the once.

One of the many times I cross-examined him regarding my sister, he spoke of how meeting my mother had freed him of his sexual anxieties. She'd saved him, he said. As for my sister, in the months since her attempted suicide, he'd combed through his past actions, he said, looking for ways he might have contributed to her desire to die.

I could hear my sister's voice in my head, her insistence he'd done something to her, something too terrible to remember.

He'd spanked her more often, he said. 'It always struck me as odd,' he said. 'She was the quiet one, but when the two of you got playing together and I had work to finish – some deadline looming – more often than not, Christina gave the shout that made me lose my temper, she'd cross the line, keep going after I'd given my warnings. You, on the other hand, seemed to know exactly when to put the brakes on. You had an uncanny ability to read me. You'd go quiet in the nick of time. And so it was Christina I'd take over my knee.'

≈

Christina and I were playing, and from the depths of our game we heard our father's voice call from the next room, demanding quiet. Briefly his displeasure hung in the air. We did not quiet our play. Our game grew wilder. As the volume of our voices swelled, the rumble of our father's discontent darkened the afternoon. His requests hardened into commands; they hailed down, but we dodged them. 'If I have to ask again, there will be consequences.' 'Keep this up, and one of you will get a spanking.' The air in the room had changed temperature. We played on, running, shouting, ignoring the storm, which was sure to pass.

Did I watch while he spanked her? If I concentrate on the idea of me bearing witness, a picture comes. I see a girl lying, face down, over his knees. But is she me or Christina?

The carpet has become my world view; his hand descends, slaps the cloth of my skirt, or the cloth of my pants, and the heat that spreads through my body is a heat of anger and shame. Anger ignites in my head and belly. This anger I aim at him. And I aim it at me for bringing his rage down upon me. I feel no physical pain. His hand is not hitting hard. But words hammer. They add confusion to my condition. He does not want to be doing what he is doing, he declares. By not listening when told to be quiet, I have left him no choice – so his pummelling words insist. His palpable turmoil travels through me in waves. That I am being punished for not having stopped my noise when asked to do so by my father, I accept. But that I am to blame for the anguish that spanking me inspires in him – this is unfair. His anguish is borderless. It enters me and frightens me.

Sometimes the girl over his knees is me, other times my sister.

I suspect that being spanked wounded Christina more deeply than me. I imagine it wounded her differently. Not only was she put over our father's knees more often (if he remembered correctly), but for her the punishment came unannounced. Her focus on our game was too complete to let in his warnings. His mounting irritation failed to shift her attention from our play. The moment to obey arrived and went unnoticed. The shock of the unannounced – our father's voice, then his hand – put a violent end to her delight, tore the fabric of her world. When I was the one he spanked, I'd heard him threaten and I knew what I was in for.

'There is no blue. There is only out of the blue,' she would write decades later in her journal.

≈

When we are small and on holiday with our mother, visiting her parents outside Boston, our father not with us – a mountain of work, a list of deadlines, keeping him in Toronto – still spanking occurs. In a letter to him, our mother writes:

> Dearest Darling,
> ... Last night, Martha, who did not want to go to bed, and made a great fuss, got a spanking ...

Spanking, it would seem, was performed by either parent and regarded as a sound component of child-rearing.

≈

It occurs on the stone terrace behind the house. Christina is seven or perhaps younger. From our costume box, she's selected and pulled over her body a dress made of shiny maroon fabric. Long ago, when our mother was a child, the dress had belonged to her. It ends, on Christina, mid-calf. Below it her blue jeans protrude. On her head flops a hat made of limp black velvet. It resembles an upside-down pudding and is a cast-off, abandoned by one of our grandmothers.

Several neighbourhood children have dropped by. They wear ordinary clothing. Perhaps my sister and I were playing dress-up when the others arrived. But if I too was earlier in disguise, I've since taken off my costume. Only Christina remains dressed up. We are interrupted by my father, who bursts through the back door of the house. 'Don't you ever do that again,' he shouts. Without further explanation he takes Christina over his knees and spanks her through her silk and denim. She does not cry. She makes no sound. Equally silent are the other children as they witness her humiliation. When our father has punished his daughter, and in so doing released his rage, he goes back inside and our game resumes. Or is our game over?

What was it Christina had done? Did she know? What had our father discovered indoors to ignite his fury? How could he have named Christina the culprit, responsible for whatever crime he'd uncovered, unless he'd been informed by our mother?

Were this scene not a memory but a video on my iPhone, I'd delete it. I'd delete my sister's public humiliation and her mute acceptance of her fate. I'd delete this evidence of our father's capacity for rage, a capacity I share. I'd delete that day on the terrace so it wouldn't translate my beloved father into the father my sister came to hate. Or claimed to hate. Until his death, in her thirty-fifth year, she would send him, now and again, a letter full of friendly discourse.

≈

She does not raise her head. Uninterested in being photographed, or unaware of the photographer (our father), she pursues her inspection of the soapy liquid in the cup she holds. She is preparing to blow the filmy substance through the ring at the end of her plastic stick. Now a delicate bubble is forming and about to break free. On its taut surface shimmer the many colours concealed within a ray of light.

Numerous snapshots, taken of us when we were small, show Christina absorbed in an exploration of her choosing: blowing a soap bubble, turning the pages of a book, attending to a doll's pressing needs, or examining some object hidden from the camera's lens.

When we stand side by side, posing, as we've been asked or told to do, she meets the camera with an oddly empty stare, whereas I laugh, or glare, aiming all my ardour at the person holding the small apparatus that is about to capture me, both wanting and not wanting to be captured. Christina's expression suggests she is far away, her emotions unavailable, her mind elsewhere, the camera's intrusion a rupture, a shock.

The shots that show her eyes full of absence she presented to Dr. R as evidence. But Dr. R did not see in them what Christina saw.

'Look, I told Dr. R, look at the lack of affect in this child's face. How can you tell me she's not being abused? Clearly I'm traumatized. It's there in my face. But Dr. R doesn't believe in my past. She refuses to see it.'

I suggested she try changing psychiatrists. As if doing so were as easy as changing socks. I offered to help find her someone new. 'No,' she said. 'Dr. R is smart. I'm unlikely to find another shrink as intelligent as her. I can catch her out sometimes, but she's pretty smart, we're well matched.'

Last week, yet again, I pulled the photos from the drawer of my desk and pondered the look of absence in my sister's eyes, asking myself whose interpretation of that look I should trust.

Now and again, when Christina and I met for coffee, or when she perched on a stool in my kitchen while I cooked us dinner, or when I stood in her doorway, unsure how far to enter, she'd tell me she wondered if she was born somewhere on the autism spectrum. 'That would explain some of it,' she'd say. 'When I first read about Temple Grandin's hug machine, I wanted one. I imagined how wonderful it would be to be held without being touched by a Human. Maybe I'm autistic and always have been, but it went unnoticed.'

≈

Our mother, the artist with the keen and subtle eye, the woman whose seemingly effortless elegance makes heads turn, has chosen Shoe A for her eleven-year-old daughter, who rejects Shoe A. No amount of explaining the merits of Shoe A can convince Christina to favour Shoe A. Already her heart is set on Shoe B. Until now, beauty has been our mother's to define. When finding fault with Christina's taste fails to dissuade her from desiring Shoe B, our mother resorts to expressing sadness and disappointment. When maternal disappointment does not alter Christina's choice of shoe, our mother drops all resistance and becomes admiring of Shoe B.

As battles over clothing erupted, how conscious were our mother's manoeuvres, her shifting responses to Christina's determined efforts to define herself, to seek autonomy by way of footwear and anything she wore over her body?

I've lived so long with my sister's conviction that our mother was calculating. Yet I'm more inclined to see our mother as having acted blindly, from a place of fear, unaware of the depth of her desire to control her daughter. As urgent as her hunger to control her was her hunger to please her. The more ardently Christina strove to impose a gap between herself and our mother, the more frantically our mother attempted to close the gap.

≈

As for our father, he increasingly found fault with his teen-aged daughter. Her understanding of social mores was diverging. His views she dismissed as absurdly outdated and unjustifiable. What difference did it make, she argued, if she knew someone's last name or only their first? If she met someone called Cathy or Pete and had no interest in learning their surname, what was wrong with that? And why should her father take offence? A surname, he explained, tells you what family a person comes from. A surname, he insisted, was of significance. Born in 1915, he'd been formed in a different world. He resented having his daughter jettison his values, no matter how minor. She lacked experience; he was her elder. They fought over the significance of surnames, over the dangers of tobacco, over how the words *fuck* and *shit*, erupting from a girl's mouth, could alter how she was perceived, and whether this was fair, and what should be done about it.

Did Christina really want to be seen as a 'loose woman'? She was welcome to argue for gender equality – a form of justice he fully endorsed – but not when it came to cursing. She was welcome to excel at school and aim to become a translator or a professor, but her refusal to accept his warning, that by cursing she'd invite men to treat her with disrespect, showed her lack of understanding of how the world worked. No, she insisted, it was he who no longer understood how the world worked. She was free to say *fuck* or *shit* as often as she liked. Many adults more willing than he was to accept social change saw nothing wrong with girls using the same vocabulary as boys. He was fully in favour of justice for girls and women, but he did not see how society would be improved by having girls and women add to the vulgarity produced by boys and men.

Their arguments would end with Christina pushing back her chair and running up the stairs to her room.

In the silence that followed the slam of her daughter's door, our mother would rebuke her husband for his insensitivity. She would not suggest that he show more respect for Christina's thinking, that he admit that his own opinions were merely opinion, but rather she'd point to Christina's fragility. While they argued over Christina, I'd knock my spoon against my plate, then come up with a story to distract them from their disagreement. I'd make a silent vow never to resemble my sister, neither in her supposed fragility nor in her determination to challenge our father. I did not see her as fragile but mysterious. What compelled her to poke holes in our father's logic escaped me. I preferred peace to logic. Seeing the world through my father's eyes felt safe, or had felt safe until the start of the disputes that went in circles, turning our family into a dog chasing its own tail.

One evening, my father informed my sister that she owed him respect whether she agreed with his opinions or not. Did she answer him with a silent glare? Perhaps he repeated that those with more life experience had something to teach her. Perhaps she declared this unfair, since he would always exceed her in experience and could therefore use his age to win, however flawed his thinking. Perhaps, she further stated, lowering her eyes (or meeting his gaze), his argument was illogical, and didn't he always say that what he wanted from his daughters was logic? Perhaps, exhilarated by her own logic, she informed him that since she was being logical, surely he should respect her, regardless of her age. Perhaps he, cornered by her superior logic, lashed out, declaring that once she'd fought in a war and defended her country, her opinions might weigh more. Perhaps she, now on the edge of tears, hissed that there was no war for her to fight except inside this house, and therefore no way for her to receive his respect, and that he was placing her in an impossible position.

Years later, she'd summarize: 'He extolled the virtues of debate but was a poor loser. I displayed the intelligence he claimed to encourage, only to receive his disapproval and anger.'

He had not only infuriated but lacerated her.

$$\approx$$

At fifteen, to think about what my seventeen-year-old sister was doing to herself in private with a razor or a broken bottle felt as dangerous as walking into the middle of an open field during a lightning storm, and so I avoided such thinking.

Not until I was in my early twenties would a delayed bolt of lightning strike and jolt me off my feet. I was walking along a busy sidewalk with a friend who was recounting that her older sister, who lived in New York, was going through a rough spell, and that she hoped to go visit her soon. Yes, I nodded. My sister too. She's gone through rough spells. As the words formed in my mind, they acquired an electric charge, and I crumpled. An inexplicable exhaustion overcame me. I sat on the sidewalk, crying.

In a letter postmarked Victoria, BC, June 2, 1991, sent to me
by Christina in the year she turned thirty-three, she wrote of
a recent bad dream from which she'd woken whining:

I was being mercilessly – really cruelly – tickled by
a man in an extremely ticklish spot just below my
left ribs; I was trying to scream but couldn't; all
my muscles had cramped up in an effort to resist
the tickling; I could barely breathe, I felt as if I
were choking and suffocating all at once – and all
I could think of was that I wanted to say 'Don't!'
but couldn't – and finally I woke up still trying to
say it, but just whining instead.

This was obviously a version of a molestation
dream – any guesses who the man was? – but it also
reminded me of a strange memory I have of Donald
putting me in one of those green duffle bags we
used to have at Loon Island, and tickling me through
the bag; it was all a big joke to him … (I have several
memories of Donald tickling me until I was in a
complete physical panic, without the duffle bag –
all of them at Loon Island. Do you have any similar
memories? It really nauseates me how many tip-of-
the-iceberg dreams I have of Donald; sometimes I
wish I could find a good therapist and thrash it all
out; but for the most part I'd rather not disrupt my
life that way at this point – and unfortunately my
previous experiences with psychiatrists – and mostly
psychotherapists – have left me with a deep distrust
of the profession.

There is one thing it's never occurred to me to
tell you about, which involves Donald indirectly; I

don't know if I should tell you about it in a letter – perhaps you know about it already. I've tried to write several stories about it – three or four of them – but never succeeded; which shows that I still have a hard time dealing with the experience – which was this: that when I was 13, in Grade 8, Mr. S, the janitor, used to come on to me sexually. (I feel a bit like passing out as I write this). He never raped me or anything; but he used to kiss me hard on the lips and hold me really tight, and show me pornographic pictures in tabloids he kept in his janitorial room in the basement ... I remember riding home on the bus one day, telling myself that what was going on was a 'good thing' because we were two lonely people helping one another out – or some such disgusting nonsense; essentially I was trying to believe that he 'needed me' – that I wasn't just a body to him ... Eventually someone must have seen us together, because one afternoon Mrs. V, the school secretary, came downstairs when I was standing just inside the door of the janitor's cubicle, and told me angrily to come upstairs at once, and that I was never to go near Mr. S's room again. (Thus, of course, laying the blame on me rather than Mr. S) ... Dear Martha, I hope this hasn't upset you. Perhaps, as I said, you already knew about it; perhaps it comes as an ugly surprise ... To me it points to the fact cited in several incest books I've leafed through: that girls who are molested at home as children are often approached by 'secondary molesters' as well – neighbours, uncles, whatever ... Boy what a cheerful letter! ... we're having a beautiful spring in Victoria; I'm feeling pretty good about everything except the past.

Casting the janitor, Mr. S, in the role of 'secondary molester,' whose prey our father had prepared her to become, made our father partially responsible for what had occurred in the janitor's room. Of the deeply unjust shame and self-blame that surfaced whenever she recalled Mr. S molesting her and heard (in memory) the school secretary reprimanding her for hanging out with Mr. S, she could partially cleanse herself by holding our father accountable for what the janitor had done – for what she'd 'let happen' because of our father.

The true culprit was Mr. S, her molester.

Yet I can connect by a dotted line our father's way of interacting with Christina in her adolescence to her difficulty rejecting the sexual advances of Mr. S.

A thirteen-year-old girl, who has recently taken to challenging her father's authority, and whose confidence is being ground down by his angry reactions, finds a more accepting, a more tender paternal figure in the form of Mr. S, a warm and even-tempered middle-aged man, much liked by students and staff. Briefly she basks in the friendship offered by this person she can please – she who has ceased to please her own father, and he her.

When Mr. S comes on to her sexually, dropping the role of father, she does not dare resist. How can she fairly refuse what he suggests she's invited? She excites him, he tells her. How pretty she is, as pretty as the women in his porno tabloids. It all feels wrong. But the wrong, she's being told, is her doing, and to reject him would place her further in the wrong.

Her reluctance to stop visiting him, for fear of hurting his feelings, speaks of her relationship to male authority. It reveals an understanding absorbed from home and from the broader world that females are responsible for men's emotions. Our father needn't have molested her to have taught her to accept responsibility for the emotions of men, and for our mother to have taught the same lesson by example.

Could the unidentified man tickling her mercilessly in her dream have been, I now ask myself, that creepy boyfriend she had in her third year of university, the one who showed her, she told me, snapshots of every woman he'd screwed? He kept them in an album. 'How could you keep going out with him?' I asked when she described the album and the way he'd tickle her until she screamed or started choking in her panic. She answered me by laughing, and in her laugh was the hardness of someone who's been hurt and who has learned to derive a certain power from her ability to withstand emotional pain by stepping outside herself.

To learn now, to learn again, from her letter, that our father tickled her when she was a child does not surprise me.

I wanted his tickling and went looking for it. When I'd wake, at Loon Island, I'd run to our parents' room, where our father lay on his back. I'd climb the mountain of his legs, perch on the summit formed by his knees, then hurl myself down onto his chest, eager to have his fingers run up and down my sides before I escaped his clutches, eager to squeal and laugh as I ascended the leg mountain once more, and again threw myself into the cage of his arms.

What delighted one daughter frightened the other.

Climb into this duffle bag, he proposed. Then he transformed into the monster tickler. He failed to hear her panic. Caught up in a game he imagined to be harmless, a game that gave him pleasure, he did not ask if her protests, uttered between squeals of seeming excitement and danger-infused delight, might mean she was not experiencing happiness. Or were her protests mute?

He playfully taught her to fear him. He did so unaware that the fear he instilled would outlast the game. He would have grieved had he woken to what he'd done. He, my beloved and well-intentioned father. But absence of malevolence did not diminish the harm caused. To have her cries for help rejected, repeatedly misunderstood, rooted feelings of helplessness in her body. His harmless game seeded in her a sense that her reality was opaque to others. Others, she increasingly imagined as she grew, were better able than her to communicate with one another. Others existed in a separate and enviable realm from which she was barred. Others enjoyed the freedom of mutual comprehensibility, whereas she inhabited, looking back to her childhood, the imposed and stifling darkness of a canvas duffle bag. Inside this darkness her terror was met with laughter, and her body's agony delighted in by her father.

From the intense emotions of childhood, from our earliest sense-making, springs our adult anticipation of what we can expect from the world.

≈

The school secretary, Mrs. V., telephoned our mother. She expressed concern that Christina, more than once, had been noticed sleeping under a staircase when she ought to have been in class.

Our mother, many years later, would confess to me a deep regret. Christina had asked for permission to change schools. She'd done so around the time Mrs. V called to say that Christina had been found sleeping under the stairs. Our mother refused to allow my sister to leave the small school she and I had entered as young children and to discover on her own something new: life in a large public high school.

Of the janitor, Mr. S, our mother said nothing. I was in my early twenties at the time of our conversation and had not yet learned from Christina about Mr. S, so I made no mention of him either.

'Why did you refuse to let her change?' I asked. Our mother replied that she'd been frightened. 'Christina seemed so lost, already, in a small and familiar school. Someplace larger, more anonymous, anything could have happened to her, and how would I have known?'

5

All that I said, or wrote, Christina dismantled in search of evidence.

In my novel *The Search for Heinrich Schlögel*, I decided to send a German teenager to Baffin Island in 1980, and, once I got him there, upend how time functioned for him and him alone. Heinrich, my protagonist, liked to walk and was a slow reader. This he and I had in common. Unlike me, he was fascinated by animals and insects and since childhood had filled notebooks with the details of their lives: hedgehogs, whales, butterflies, snails. Like me, he had an older sister he greatly admired, who was both a talented linguist and suicidal.

To better evoke Heinrich's youth in rural Germany, I turned to my friend Iris and asked her to describe her hometown of Tettnang. The two of us seated at a large table, I waited for her to divulge her childhood. Her silence deepened, then she took hold of a paper napkin and urgently drew a map. The route she'd cycled to school as a child appeared. A tiny dark square indicated the barn where the bullies hung out. Suddenly she was pedalling fast, then faster and faster to escape a possible ambush. Next came a steep hill her parents had warned her to descend cautiously since trucks careened along it. Always she'd slow to a halt in front of the butcher's. The look of fear in the eyes of the steer waiting in the field beside the shop made her tremble, and the anguish of his lowing she'd carry with her to school, where it would fill her ears, drowning out the recitation of multiplication tables and historical dates. On her map she included a castle perched on a hill overlooking a ravine where migrant workers lived, mostly Italians and Turks, whom she was told ate hedgehogs and might therefore eat her were she to venture into the ravine. Her house bordered a hops field. Regularly the hops were drenched in bird-murdering pesticides. Out the back door she'd slip to collect the unbreathing feathered bodies.

From her bedroom window, if she leaned far enough on a clear day, she could see out of Germany, all the way to Switzerland. Seeing beyond Germany allowed her to breathe better.

She told me of farmers riding high on their huge, modern tractors. From such an elevation they could not see the fawns nestled in the tall grass below. Every spring, the blades of the giant machines would deprive a few fawns of their legs.

All that Iris offered I included in my novel, the manuscript of which I gave to Christina, warning her that in Heinrich's sister I'd tried to create a version of her.

Several days later she returned the manuscript. 'I had to stop,' she said, 'when I came to the part about the fawns and the tractors. I'm sorry, but I couldn't keep going after that. What I did read, from the start until I had to stop, was good. The scene in the hospital, after Inge tries to kill herself, is well done. You've aestheticized my experience very well.'

Aestheticized. That was her word.

A few weeks after returning my manuscript to me, Christina knocked on my door. 'I think I've found Heinrich.' Her eyes were bright with excitement. She held out a book of photography.

The Architect's Brother, by artists Robert and Shana ParkeHarrison. I stared in wonder. The cover showed a man seen from the back, stumbling, dressed in a crumpled, ill-fitting suit, holding his arms up and out, in imitation of wings. From his gloved left hand hung a cage confining a single large bird. From the backs of both his gloved hands, clusters of strings rose into the air. The strings were tied to the feet of flapping birds, whose collective efforts were preventing him from falling in his faltering advance across an expanse of dirt. Christina and I turned the pages, discussing which of the many surreal images of the man in his crumpled suit might do best for the cover of my novel, if my publisher were to agree and the artists to grant their permission.

To her psychiatrist but not to me, Christina explained that my mention of fawns having their legs severed by tractor blades indicated that I'd been forced to torture animals in my childhood, just as she'd been forced to do. Our parents, and the ring of pedophiles to which they belonged, had learned from the Nazis that forcing your victims to perform acts of torture on others reduces their willingness to divulge the unbearable cruelties to which they themselves have been subjected.

≈

Survival dictated that Christina keep all Humans at bay. Survival demanded invisibility. Yet to locate herself required that she be seen. If the sensation of existing, and the conviction that we exist, requires that we be witnessed, then we must find a witness or cease to believe that we are real. She chose language as her witness.

To her fridge door she taped a message that read: 'Language believes in the patient, in the patient's real existence within language as one of its aspects,' and these inscribed words literally saw her, thereby making her real, she explained.

By language she could bear being seen. To be – this meant to be '*made up of & made-up (maddened – up) by language.*'

In her journal she wrote:

LANGUAGE BELIEVES IN THE PATIENT, IN THE PATIENT'S REAL EXISTENCE WITHIN LANGUAGE AS ONE OF ITS ASPECTS. How can someone who has a message as true as this one in their life, think of what humans refer to as 'love' as anything but risible. (Unkind? I – just as humans do – know only what I know. Humans aren't my strong point, any more than I am theirs. Nothing wrong with natural ignorance. Distance is the only thing: without it no survival.

In her journal she wrote:

Robot. I am an invisible robot; as everyone inside my head knows, as no one on the outside – naturally – knows. There are around 87–97 of us; each has a separate function, or subfunction within a group. Lots of groups, subgroups; this is essential to invisibility maintenance. Groups of 6 to 9 come and go through our pseudo-human consciousness; those leaving brief those arriving. These temporary groups are picked for their complementary skills.

Lately my armpits have been itching – someone has been trying to sell me on the idea that diseased wings are trying to set up shop there – to implant themselves, to supply spy tools (cameras in hatpinheads, etc. ...), to whom, even the persuaders can't say.

To avoid being seen, pinned down, tortured, destroyed, fragment yourself, she advised: '*Lots of groups, subgroups; this is essential to invisibility maintenance.*'

She: a theatre of action.

Her selves: an ongoing act of guerrilla warfare.

In her journal she wrote:

> I can't produce writing that locates anything. I feel unlocatable, or located briefly, peremptorily, in some meaning vessel outside myself – for instance, when un(der)medicated I experience myself as some random inanimate thing that has 'stolen my brain' & is controlling me from a distance with its own cruel purposes in mind.

In her journal she wrote:

> Randomness pulls: & something pulls back. I am the something, but am also its attraction to randomness: or how the random is drawn ineluctably to it, how the random always finds it (me) out.

She points to the self as both resistance and attraction. We wish (in equal measure?) to dissolve into and to separate from the chaos that birthed us.

The self becomes manifest, then slips away, fleeting as any utterance. We are returned to infinite possibility, to the as-yet-unmade.

In her journal she wrote:

> The proof that I exist is in the transitions from utterly random – in the sense that it is always roiling around

– language potential, into whatever utterances I am: am making: these ams. I am (what makes) these transits I am. Language potential, unmanifest, infinite; its potentates. Taters, ate, potent. The linguophagous am.

Phagous: eating, feeding on, devouring.

Linguophagous: she who feeds on language.

If she who feeds on language exists solely as language, does she disappear by feeding on herself?

≈

Not only through language did Christina situate herself. It was not her sole material of self-location. Paint, yarn, cloth, wire, lead weights (fallen from the wheels of trucks), stuffed animals, armless mannequins. Her installations, created from found objects – clever, unsettling, informed by the art of those she admired most: Louise Bourgeois, Joseph Beuys, Francis Bacon – spread from room to room.

Shit and piss were her materials too – excreted bodily extensions of language. In the presence of her *Shitcoil* paintings, she felt more 'real.'

Her secret delight, her hidden revenge on Humans, was to carry her warm shit, her fragrant gold, in a Starbucks coffee cup down the street, in and out of bookstores, in and out of libraries, in and out of her psychiatrist's office.

In her journal she notes:

carrying wet shit past Bible pushers
carrying wet shit through H&M

In her journal she documents:

10:30 p.m. peed on shirt
4:05 a.m. peed on shirt
9:08 a.m. peed on shirt
10:57 a.m. peed on shirt
10: 59 a.m. shat on canvas
4:10 p.m. peed on shirt
4:42 p.m. peed on shirt
4:43 p.m. painted EUGEN on shirt
6:55 p.m. shat on canvas
5: 57 p.m. pee-saturated EUGEN shirt
            transferred to hanger to dry

The shirt had been worn, long ago, by our mother to keep her clothes clean while painting.

Eugen. Eugenics.

Eugene: the name of our mother's autistic uncle. He'd worked flipping hamburgers in Grand Rapids, Michigan, and from the daily newspapers cut and saved cartoons. Our mother, who did not live in Grand Rapids, was taken infrequently, in her childhood, to visit her uncle. Yet she felt an affection for him that would stay with her all her life. 'He loved the funnies, and so I loved him.'

In her journal Christina wrote:

at roughly 9:13 – 9:17 a.m.
                        patient paints shitcoil
                        gold white glue mixes
                        with gold paint to
                        make shit adhere
          patient's 2nd shitcoil
                  gives off unholy reek
                      so can't be dried under a
                          ceiling fan so takes

                    days to dry
                        patient
                    doesn't mind this
      what overrides displeasure
                    in a truly nasty stench
                        is pleasure in the shitcoil's
                            presence as an undeniable
                            situatable reality
10:48 a.m. stench has   subsided enough so that
shitcoil on   canvas can be moved to under a
ceiling   fan (window ajar)
shitcoil has been turned over since underside
is still wet

first phone photos (2) of   both shitcoils
pleasure   in shitcoil project
          is also in its secrecy

also note:

                    pleasure in shitcoils as an
                    authentic refusal-response to
                    the   human refusal of schizophrenic
                    language as 'non-communicative.'

In her journal she wrote:

(for depression; I'm on meds – 600–750 mg. Sero-
quel nightly, in the morning 10 mg. Prozac, to be
raised to 20 mg. if it doesn't give me bad side effects,
as Wellbutrin and – worse – Ciraplex both did).
Then I bought an unsweetened vegan pumpkin pie
and headed home on the TTC (public transit). Twice
in the Spadina subway station when I was alone I
looked at my shitcoils phone photos. I re-read what

I've written so far. I saw a coil of human hair, a hair-coil on the back of a head, that reminded me of a plump shitcoil. (I broke my glasses – deliberately – sometime around last Christmas, and everything that's farther than 2 feet or so from me is blurred; I have no intention of fixing my glasses since I like the way electric lights blur, I like to blur humans around me.

≈

Title: *Shit Face*.

Materials: shit, white glue, gold paint.

Dimensions: unknown (destroyed by the artist, Christina Baillie, in 2017).

Likely Christina knew of Piero Manzoni, who canned his excrement in 1961, labelling each tin *Artist's Shit*. He too equated his excrement with gold and sold one of his cans to an art collector for its weight in the precious metal. Thirty grams of shit for thirty grams of gold.

From the Tate gallery these words by artist and critic Jon Thompson:

> The *Merda d'artista*, the artist's shit, dried naturally and canned 'with no added preservatives', was the perfect metaphor for the bodied and disembodied nature of artistic labour: the work of art as fully incorporated raw material, and its violent expulsion as commodity. Manzoni understood the creative act as part of the cycle of consumption: as a constant reprocessing, packaging, marketing, consuming, reprocessing, packaging, *ad infinitum*.

The pressure placed on artists to subject their work to 'violent expulsion as commodity' Christina had long found repellent. She'd long ago declared to a friend and fellow writer: 'I hate what happens when society and art meet – not only the way society treats artists, but what I've always seen as artists' complicity in the relationship.'

≈

In part, Christina's use of excrement in her art was a response to 'the human refusal of schizophrenic language as "non-communicative."'

Christina told Dr. R that all her poetry was written in code.

Dr. R stated (how often?) that her poetry was (therefore?) 'non-communicative.'

More than once, when we met over coffee, Christina voiced her anger and sorrow that Dr. R took 'no interest' in her writing.

Knowing that the limitation was Dr. R's, not her own, did not spare her from feeling cut to the quick, she said.

≈

Frequent failures of communication with Humans plagued Christina. One day, she recommended that I read *I Love Dick*, a novel by Chris Kraus. When I reported, the following week, that the book did not speak to me, that it rubbed me the wrong way, but that doubtless my response said as much about me as it did about *I Love Dick*, she quickly asked that we change the subject. My response had upset her. To what degree I would not know until after her death, when I read in her journal:

My sister is angered by Chris Kraus this saddens
me or no it sort of deadens my responses to life
it saps me of my responsiveness
    THERE IS NO POSSIBILITY OF COMMUNICATION
    THERE IS NO POSSIBILITY OF CONJUNCTION

The above pronouncement she later copied from her journal onto the inside of a book cover, using her manual typewriter. Several book covers, much-typed-upon, she stapled
together to form a scroll. Soon she'd created several scrolls,
then several more.

≈

Inside the *Dear Martha* binder, waiting for me to find it
or not:

A description of a strategy that got her 'through & past
a bout of suicidality.'

Suddenly there it was, after her death: a depiction of
how to survive.

First she stuffed a pillow into a pair of our mother's old
stockings. To this creation she gave the pronoun 'she,' and
named her 'Just Shush,' then she pinned in place a 'birth
certificate' – a tag declaring 'New Materials Only.' Her
creation now certified-free-of-the-past, she tied its/her legs
behind her own neck and descended a set of stairs, climbed
them, and again descended, the hanging bundle of cloth
bouncing against her, its rhythmic contact bringing her
back – returning her to her body. And later, as she lay in
bed, inspecting a 'wonky inner seam' of the 'supersilky
supersheened' old hosiery, holding it up, peering in
'through sheer. Sheerest faux silk. Sheerest mesh,' her 'shattered mind' began to focus, and later still, imposing a
pattern of three-word sentences to further contain and

soothe her mind, she recorded on paper how she'd side-stepped death for now:

This three word. Format brings me. Brings me back. Yesterday was suicidal. I was yesterday. Upped my meds. Stuffed a pillow. Plump white square. Into old hosiery. Old supersilky supersheened. Palest ivory hose. Gave her a. A birth certificate. NEW MATERIALS ONLY. An old tag. Pinned tag on. Tied the legs. Legs looped I. Around my neck. Bounced her down. Bounced her up. Walked with her. Down stairs up. She swung twisted. In place swung. She her own. Own place making. Marking it out. Tu Fu her. Name or her. Name Just Shush. She is wordless. With her I. Her I on. The bed lie. She on my. Belly legs round. My neck still. I lift her. I peer in. In through sheer. Sheerest faux silk. Sheerest mesh I. Through peer at. Wonky inner seams. Rough white seams. In flat twists. By this could. Be guided I. Am in fact.

≈

From one of her journals this draft of a letter:

Dear Dr. R, Thank you for lending me the small blue dinosaur to keep me company while you are away on vacation. You are away on holiday. I miss you. The little dinosaur is helping. I'm working up my courage to introduce him to some of the others, to Lilac (the stuffed bear that belonged to a dog but was rescued by me from the branches of a Lilac tree) and Bebot, my red, devil robot, with a key that winds him up. But so far Little blue Dinosaur has only me, and I have him until you return.

≈

She was seeing Dr. R weekly for talk therapy, and to carefully monitor the effects of the medications she was taking. Many Toronto shrinks only prescribed medication for schizophrenic patients and offered no talk therapy, said Christina. She was lucky to have found Dr. R, she said, and to have convinced such a sought-after psychiatrist to take her on. To reach Dr. R's office, situated on a side street in the city's east end, she'd walk for well over an hour. Subway platforms made suicide too tempting. Buses and streetcars confined her. She preferred to walk.

≈

Location 1. Memory of a photo.

In the heat of summer, we've pulled on woollen hats and scarves, Christina and I, and our father and our mother. We are dancing on the acorn-strewn lawn in front of the house to celebrate the existence of a sunny afternoon in June. We toss our joy in the air to see where it lands.

Location 2. Body memory.

I'm riding on my father's shoulders through the woods; the horizon tilts to the rhythm of his steps. My small fingers grip his forehead. His large hands secure my ankles. Between the trees the lake shimmers.

Location 3. Body memory.

We have returned to the city. He crouches on the lawn, collecting fallen twigs, filling cardboard boxes with kindling. 'Here's a task a small person can do.' I too crouch, gather up twigs. He straightens, sends his gaze into the rustling canopy above. His eyes follow the audacious reach of an ancient oak branch, and he confides, 'In another life, if I have one, I'd like to be a squirrel and jump from branch to branch, way up there.' I too straighten, and my eyes follow the squirrel he'll become, in its running leaps.

Location 4: Body memory.

I have grown, years have elapsed, and again summer. He shows me where to place my foot to brace the log, as I draw the saw toward me, then glide it away. Never use force. Make the sawing sing, the work smooth. But if the blade catches, if the wood presses in, if it binds the metal, stop. Extract the blade with care.

Location 5. Lavender dress.

A lavender dress on a fifteen-year-old girl. Or was she twelve? Our father looked up from his paper and said to Christina, as she paused in the front hall, 'That dress looks fetching, it shows off your womanly shape.' It was a shirt dress, short-sleeved, a simple dress with buttons down the front. She ignored him, closed the door behind her, walked out into the world. He returned his attention to his newspaper. But I'd heard the tenderness and admiration in his voice. His tone needled me. I envied her. Through the window I watched her disappear up the long street, and I vowed to be unwomanly.

≈

W, or the Memory of a Childhood is the title of a slender book by French novelist Georges Perec, a writer I've long wanted to read but avoided until recently, because the novel he's best known for, *Life: A User's Manual*, is lengthy and I am a slow reader. A few months ago, a friend, eager that I read something by Perec, recommended that I try *W*.

The book's chapters alternate between descriptions of a fascistic society devoted to competitive sports (of peculiar sorts), located on the Island of W, invented by the author at the age of twelve, and the author's narration of his mostly forgotten childhood, which he attempts to piece together from his aunt's recollections, the testimony of classmates, a handful of photographs, and his own meagre memories.

Perec was born March 7, 1936, to Jewish Polish parents, recent emigrants to Paris. At the outset of World War II, Perec's father, keen to demonstrate his patriotism, enlisted in the French army. Soon a roadside explosion killed him. Perec's mother found work in an alarm clock factory. At the age of six, Perec was taken by his mother to the Gare de Lyon, where she placed him in the care of a Red Cross convoy moving children to the 'free' zone. He would spend the rest of the war in a boarding school near Grenoble run by nuns.

Though his mother was given the Paris address of a smuggler who might provide her with false papers, on the day she knocked on the smuggler's door nobody answered, and she did not return a second time. As the widow of a fallen French soldier, she'd be safe, she reassured herself. But soon the authorities took her to Drancy, then to Auschwitz, where she was murdered.

Perec's first winter at boarding school, an accident occurred. A speeding toboggan veered off course and struck Perec, who was skating with classmates. His fall on the ice broke his shoulder blade, which could not be put in a plaster cast, so the doctor bent his arm and tied it behind his back to prevent his shoulder blade from moving. One sleeve of his coat hung empty, as if he were an amputee. The special attention he received from teachers and classmates greatly comforted him in his pain.

Decades later Perec returned to the region to visit a friend in a village not far from the boarding school he'd attended as a child. By chance he was introduced to a stonemason, a man his own age, who had gone to the same school. Though neither of them remembered each other, they both recalled another boy, with whom the stonemason was still in regular contact. The stonemason asked Perec if he'd been present on the day the other boy had had his shoulder blade broken in a skating accident involving a toboggan. Listening to the stonemason describe the event, Perec realized that he'd assigned a physical injury to himself that had in fact been sustained by someone else. He'd witnessed the accident but not been hurt. Recently orphaned, he'd craved the sympathy and attention given to his injured classmate. His own injuries, psychological and profound, were going unnoticed because less visible. He too had been struck and knocked over, but by history gone off course, not a toboggan.

I read Perec's revealing words, learned of how his memory had reshaped the past, and lifting my eyes from the page I looked out the window: a brick wall, and in front of the wall a tree made leafless by winter. By tomorrow, would my memory remove from existence the cluster of seedpods attached to one branch, erase their trembling in the wind, and the wind slip into oblivion, replaced by what? By a singing bird on a windless afternoon? Returning my attention to the page covered in Perec's words, I felt certain that the truth about my father and my sister – the only one available to me – had to be of my own making, and that it would never hold still.

≈

From my bookshelf I take down each book chosen for me and given to me by Christina. In these books she located us both. In them, I now hold in my hands her long-ago desire to speak with me through the voices of these authors.

Banville, John: *The Newton Letter*
Benjamin, Walter: *Walter Benjamin's Archive*
Bernhard, Thomas: *The Voice Imitator*
Brookner, Anita: *Hotel du Lac*
Enchi, Fumiko: *Masks*
Glück, Louise: *Meadowlands*
Kleinzahler, August: *The Strange Hours Travellers Keep*
Lispector, Clarice: *A Breath of Life*
Robertson, Lisa: *3 Summers*
Sheard, Sarah: *Almost Japanese*
Svendsen, Linda: *Marine Life*
Young, Patricia: *Ruin & Beauty*

≈

Inscribed within *Walter Benjamin's Archive*:

For Martha and Jonno with infinite thanks for making my life in my house possible, Christina. Dec.24, 2014.

I close the book and promise myself I won't open it again.

≈

In the dappled yard, one day, perhaps a month before her death, the sunlight, as it fell through the arms of the oak trees, invited me to relinquish what was mine, to allow her to stay in the home of our childhoods, whatever that came to mean. It was summer, the air moist and hot. Give her what she asks of you, and you will give yourself the greatest of gifts, suggested the light, made tender by the filtering foliage above. An ease spread through me. But all too fast fear returned.

≈

It was May, and cherry trees, dressed in clouds of blossom, lined the path through the public park. I pushed our mother's wheelchair, and Christina walked beside us.

That evening, in her journal she'd write:

I was taken to a park so my landlord could enjoy nature. She is ninety-nine and will die soon. She's become quite a sweet child, far less dangerous than she used to be. I'm afraid that when she dies I'll feel skinned alive. Once my life-long battle with the Soggy Dragon is over, what will I write about? How will I continue?

Love and anger: the tension between two extremes formed a taut skin that contained my sister.

Once our mother died, she would need a new skin, a new battle.

≈

Since her death, Christina has been making appearances in the public library where I work part-time as a library assistant. Always she comes in the guise of someone else.

Last week, she arrived as a teenaged girl, cradling a kitten in her arms. Banging her head against the thick glass of a window overlooking the street, she declared her desire to throw herself in front of a car unless she could first ride home in a taxi to say goodbye to her mother. Either way she would soon end her life, she told us, and then asked that we call for a taxi.

Several months ago, she dropped by the library in the body of an old man. He had a long white beard and asked for an access code to log on to one of the public computers. The code I gave him did not work. From the chair where he sat, he shouted: 'You made a mistake, I think you made a mistake.' I got up and went to him. 'Yes,' I agreed, 'I am human, therefore I make mistakes. Let me get you a different code.' While I walked back to the reference desk, he called after me: 'You have made a mistake. I'm sure you have made a mistake.' I brought him a new code and typed it in for him. A message appeared on the screen: 'An error has occurred.' No centrally generated code had ever failed me, and so I disregarded the message. Again I typed the faulty code. The bearded man (my sister) sat beside me, his glaring eyes fixed on me. He informed me: 'I am going to be a billionaire, and when I am, nobody will have a seat at my table.' He asked me: 'What's going on here? Ten years ago I'd come and use the internet with no problem. I am a paranoid schizophrenic and you have to be nice to me. I am Dr. Aaron Lebowitz and I should by now be a billionaire. I have a feeling you are picking on me. This is an anti-Semitic act. You aren't letting me use the computer because you don't like me. I curse you. You are going to die ten years before you normally would, and before dying you will suffer from terrible ulcers.' Having spoken his mind, he rose from his chair, dismissed me with a wave of his hand, and left the library, placing each foot heavily down and breathing as heavily.

But most often Christina visits the library disguised as a skinny British woman in her sixties. Her grey hair, drawn tightly back from her bony face, forms a short ponytail behind her head. Her pale blue eyes dissect and defy. Her son has been forcefully taken from her by the government. Since I am co-operating with those holding her son hostage, she does not understand how I can sleep at night. I am causing her the most corrosive of suffering, and I am doing so for the pleasure of exercising my power over her. I have the means to reunite her with her son any time I like, but I choose not to.

≈

I type *Sister Language* on the screen of the public library's catalogue and find Christina there. Author: Baillie, Christina Mary.

Body and bound book. Weeks before the bound book came into existence she fled the material world. Her body was no longer home. The physical world had become an unbearable location. *Because of Schizophrenia, because of The Juniper Tree, because of losing the house.*

≈

So much depends on a room.

At forty-five, Christina still believed that loveliness could be hers, that loveliness could be her.

January 1, 2003, she wrote:

Small Change

Small changes can become
enormous: the slightest shift
or adjustment can be our salvation.

No need to gut
the house: just reposition
a bed or table;

best to make arrangements
when no one's looking –
at night or when you're alone;

let the results become apparent
gradually (they will be more charming
if they seem unintentional).

If an adjustment fails, don't
hurry the next one; wait awhile –
perhaps a vase will topple from a shelf
shattering in an interesting way;

perhaps the love that is hell
will pass like a fever,
leaving you sweat-soaked but warm,
no longer trembling –

you will understand that while it took
all your strength, all you had to give
to move the dining room table alone, after dark

the table is now where it should have been
all along, and your room looks lovely.

NOTES

In 'A Bend in the Path':

The excerpt from the poem 'Variations on the Decomposing Fox,' from *Faunics* by Jack Davis, published by Pedlar Press, is reprinted courtesy of the author.

In 'You Can Say Goodbye':

The etymology of *property* is from the *Collins English Dictionary*, 3rd edition (HarperCollins, 1991). The definitions of *own* and *owe* are from the *Oxford School Dictionary*, 2nd edition (Oxford University Press, 1960).

The excerpt from *Bark* by Georges Didi-Huberman, translated by Samuel E. Martin, is reprinted courtesy of MIT Press.

The two excerpts from *When We Cease to Understand the World*, by Benjamin Labatut, translated by Adrian Nathan West, published by the New York Review of Books, are reprinted courtesy of the publisher.

The statement by artist and critic Jon Thompson, about Piero Manzoni's work, I found on the Tate gallery's website. It is an excerpt from *Piero Manzoni*, exhibition catalogue, Serpentine Gallery, London, 1998.

ACKNOWLEDGEMENTS

I am a twelfth-generation settler of Scottish and English ances-try, born in Tkaronto/Toronto – the Treaty Lands and Terri-tory of the Mississauga of the Credit and the traditional terri-tory of the Anishinaabeg, Wendat, Métis, and Haudenosaunee. I live and work in Tkaronto/Toronto and on family land located within the boundaries of Treaty 18, the traditional lands of the Anishinaabeg, Haudenosaunee, Tionontati, and Wendat. I thank the many First Nations, Métis, and Inuit peoples, who are the traditional stewards of Turtle Island, for their ongoing teachings, and their protection and nurturing of the lands I call home.

Thanks to *Brick: A Literary Journal* for publishing an earlier version of 'Her Body.'

To André Alexis and Alana Wilcox for brilliant editing. Work-ing with you both has been an amazing gift.

To everyone at Coach House for their dedication and hard work.

To my agent, Samantha Haywood.

To the following friends and family who generously read *There Is No Blue* at various stages and encouraged me: Jack Davis, Ralph Kolewe, Mark Abley, Emma Moss Brender, Banuta Rubess, Joanne Schwartz, Eric Woodley, Gary Barwin, Neil McCormick, Trish Baillie.

To the following friends and family who, along with those named above, came to my rescue when my sister ended her life: Anne Egger, Vid Ingelevics, Iris Haussler, Greg Sharp,

Sophie Perceval, Gregoire Holtz, Sara Angelucci, Susan Holmes, Pete Taylor, Kathy Giles, Eva H.D., Beth Follett, Stan Dragland, Howard Norman, Annie Beer, Catherine Bush, Susan Glickman, Toan Klein, Roo Borson, Kim Maltman, Brenda McComb, Marco Fonseca, Mona Philip, Dominique Denis, Marcus Schubert, Diana Liljelund, Rémy Sardou, Guy Ewing, David Dorenbaum, Kaaren Heaseman, Joel Rosenbloom, Ellen Bateman, Naomi Jaye, Ivan Jaye, Glenda Goodgol, Kay Smythe, Sandra Farias, Rodrigo Briones, Kyo Maclear, Rita Sirignano, Hamish Kerfoot, Jessica Moore, Kate Cayley, Theo Heras, Mike Hoolboom, Zab Hobart, Brian Katz, Geneviève Guillot, Paul Guering, Marie Louise et Alain Perceval, Helene et Maxime Holtz, David Gressot, Dan Diamond, Carol McLaughlin, Robert and Christa McDermott, Ilse Stockwood, Peter Wilton, Andrew Wilton, Denis Galliera, and my co-workers at the Sanderson branch of the Toronto Public Library.

To Dr. Sarah Freke for her patience and insights.

To Jonno for making my life infinitely better by being who he is.

To my courageous and inspiring daughter, Emma.

Martha Baillie lives and works in Toronto. Her novel *The Incident Report* was longlisted for the Scotiabank Giller Prize and is to be released as a feature film in 2023, directed by Naomi Jaye, starring Britt Lower and Tom Mercier, with Charlie Kaufman as executive producer. *The Search for Heinrich Schlögel* was an Oprah editors' pick. *Sister Language*, co-written with her late sister, Christina Baillie, was a 2020 Trillium Book Award finalist. Martha's non-fiction can be found in *Brick: A Literary Journal*. Her poetry has appeared in the *Iowa Review*. Her multimedia project based on *The Search for Heinrich Schlögel* is archived at www.schlogel.ca.

Typeset in Baskerville.

Printed at the Coach House on bpNichol Lane in Toronto, Ontario, on Zephyr Antique Laid paper, which was manufactured This book was printed with vegetable-based ink on a 1973 Heidelberg KORD offset litho press. Its pages were folded on a Baumfolder, gathered by hand, bound on a Sulby Auto-Minabinda, and trimmed on a Polar single-knife cutter.

Coach House is on the traditional territory of many nations, including the Mississaugas of the Credit, the Anishnabeg, the Chippewa, the Haudenosaunee, and the Wendat peoples, and is now home to many diverse First Nations, Inuit, and Métis peoples. We acknowledge that Toronto is covered by Treaty 13 with the Mississaugas of the Credit. We are grateful to live and work on this land.

Edited by André Alexis
Cover design by Zab Design and Typography, cover art *Pensive Woman* by
    Mary Jane Holmes Baillie (1941)
Interior design by Crystal Sikma
Author photo by Jonno Lightstone

Coach House Books
80 bpNichol Lane
Toronto ON M5S 3J4
Canada

416 979 2217
800 367 6360

mail@chbooks.com
www.chbooks.com